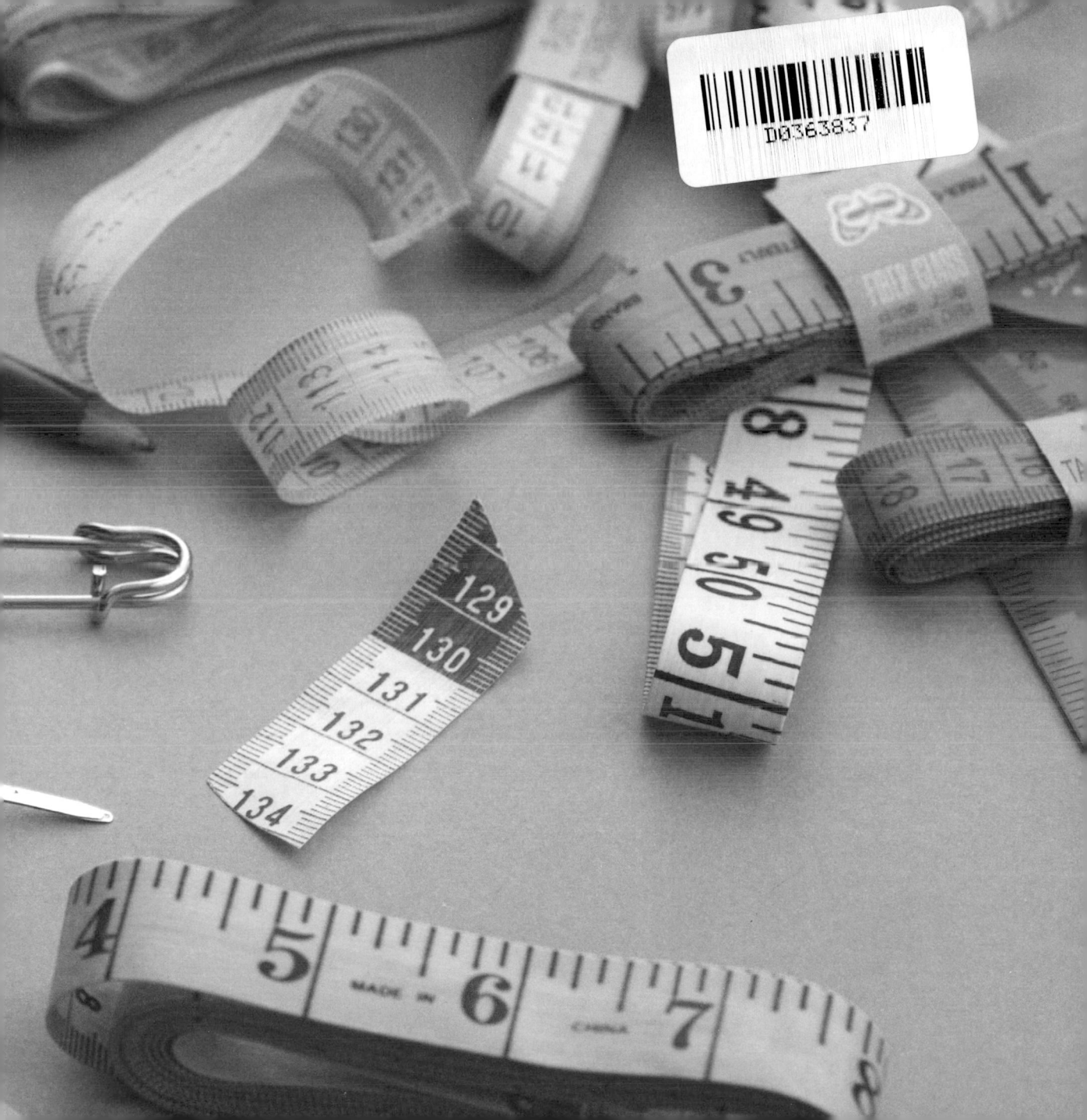

D0363837

HOW TO MAKE JEWELLERY WITH TATTY DEVINE

Disclaimer:
The information in this book has been compiled by way of general guidance in relation to making jewellery. It is not a substitute and not to be relied on for specific professional advice. Please take care when using any tools or sharp implements and ensure that the applicable manufacturer's safety guidelines are followed. The author and publisher disclaim as far as the law allows any liability arising directly or indirectly from the use or misuse of the information contained in this book.

Tatty Devine are the exclusive owners of any intellectual property and other rights in the jewellery designs and creative works contained in this book. The commercial exploitation or appropriation of these rights is strictly prohibited.

HOW TO MAKE JEWELLERY WITH TATTY DEVINE

Harriet Vine and Rosie Wolfenden

10 9 8 7 6 5 4 3 2 1

First published in 2011 by Virgin Books, an imprint of Ebury Publishing
A Random House Group Company

Copyright © Harriet Vine and Rosie Wolfenden 20111

The authors have asserted their right under the Copyright, Designs and Patents Act 1988 to be identified as the authors of this work.

Every reasonable effort has been made to contact the copyright holders of material reproduced in this book. If any have inadvertently been overlooked, the publishers would be glad to hear from them and make good in future editions any errors or omissions brought to their attention.

This book is sold subject to the condition that it shall not, by way of trade or otherwise be lent, resold, hired out, or otherwise circulated without the publisher's prior consent in any form of binding or cover other than that in which it is published and without a similar condition, including this condition, being imposed on the subsequent purchaser.

www.randomhouse.co.uk

Addresses for companies within The Random House Group Limited can be found at www.randomhouse.co.uk/offices.htm

The Random House Group Limited Reg. No. 954009

A CIP catalogue record for this book is available from the British Library

ISBN: 978-0-7535-4012-1

The Random House Group Limited supports The Forest Stewardship Council (FSC®), the leading international forest certification organisation. Our books carrying the FSC label are printed on FSC® certified paper. FSC is the only forest certification scheme endorsed by the leading environmental organisations, including Greenpeace. Our paper procurement policy can be found at www.randomhouse.co.uk/environment

FSC
www.fsc.org
MIX
Paper from responsible sources
FSC™ C004592

Designed and typeset by Nina Ziegler at Design Beckons

Printed and bound by Firmengruppe APPL, aprinta druck, Wemding, Germany

To buy books by your favourite authors and register for offers visit
www.randomhouse.co.uk

Acknowledgements 7

Introduction 10

Tools and Findings 14

In the Mood for Making 28

First things first 34

How to Make a...

Basic Necklace 36
Bow Tie Necklace 38
Leather Cuff 42
Gem Hair Band 46
Photocopy Watch Bracelet 50

Sticky stuff 53

How to Make a...

Radio Brooch 54
Glass Stopper Pendant 56
Sausage Dog Brooch 58
'Sovereign' Ring 61

How to Make...

Glitter Brooches 64
Some Blinging Clip-on Shades 66
Jigsaw Puzzle Earrings 68

Hole-y moley 71

How to Make a...

Tape Measure Rosette 72
Shrinky Necklace 77
Horse Brass Necklace 82
Musical Note Charm Bracelet 83

Drill bits and pieces 85

How to Make a...

Plectrum Bracelet and Necklace 86
Keyboard Necklace 92
Threepenny Bit Necklace 94
Wooden Mushroom Necklace 96
Tiny Fruit Machine Dice Necklace 99

Making a spectacle of yourself 103

How to Make a...

Simple Glasses Necklace 106
Pearl Glasses Necklace 108
Snazzy Sunglasses Necklace 114

A Final Word 116

Index 120

Acknowledgements

Nina Ziegler for designing this book and getting it so right

Eithne Farry for her way with words

John William for understanding what goes on in our minds

Dominic Mifsud for being such a patient photographer

Saga Sig for taking such perfect pictures of people

Hannah Knowles, our Editor, and everyone at Virgin Books and Ebury Publishing

To all our models: Becki, Irene, Amelie, Theresa, Ella, Bridie and Sami Knight hairdresser extrordinaire.

And to everyone who has ever helped, inspired and been part of the adventure so far: Ann and Roger Vine, John and Rosalind Wolfenden, Freda Smith, Joan Wolfenden, Ben Vine, Bebe Higgins, Netia Costa, Rebecca Andreae, William Wolfenden, Harry and Ned, Jack and Tom, Dan Higgins and Tony Collins.

All of Team Tatty, past present and future! You're much loved and appreciated. In no particular order: Thelma and Paul, Mark Pawson, Rachael Matthews, Louise Harries, Nervous Stephen, Joe Egg, Herve and Paul, Nicky Abrahams, Elvina Flower, Mikey, Nick Philips, Mike and Jen, Ilona, Melissa, Rebecca and Amber, Heather, Steph, Nick Pankhurst, Liela and Luke, Fancy Smith, Dino, Matt Dawson, Susanna Edwards, Zeel, Rob Ryan, Hayley, Dan Holiday, Eel Zine, Adam Wright, Amaia, Amelia, Rocky, Bev, Mimi, Little Miss Lucifer, Jo and Simon, Austin and Clare, Rachel, Sophie and Sabrina, Cleo Ferin, Alex Barrows and The Severed Limb, Rae Jones, Anna Marie, Sandy Waibl, Anat and Jet, Jacey, Antoni and Alison, Mark and Wak, Camera Obscura, Peaches, Chicks on Speed, Gilbert and George, Electrocute, Cobra Killer, Duke Spirit, Lulu Kennedy, Michael from Blow, Basso and Brooke, Barry Newman, Tai Shani, Oh My God! I Miss You, Duke of Uke, Barbara Ryan, Angharad Lewis, Robots in Disguise, Charlie le Mindu, Pil and Galia, Paul Michael, Minna Parika, Rosie Cooper, Ruth Hiki, Georgina Starr and Paul Noble, Harry Woodrow, Susanna Heron, Clyde Hopkins, Roger Ackling, Tara D'Cruz-Noble, Calvin Holbrook, Mary Hanson, Claire Catterall, Design Beckons, Bobby McGees, Skinny Girl Diet, Suburban Mousewife, Mr Ministeck, Mrs Jones, Tobin Ireland, Bob and Sally, Barry Stillwell, Verena Paloma Jabs, Ashish, Chrome Hoof, Tokyo Dragons, John Brown and Fiona, Jamie Beeden, Nils, StereoTotal, Rubbishmen, Hilary at the French House, Rollergirls, Supermarket Sarah, Miss High Leg Kick and Richard Hutt, Bishi, Pippa Brooks, Victoria Woodcock, Emily Beaver, Blue Firth, Jamie J, Jeremy Deller, Princess Julia, Scottee, Philip Gwyn Jones, Ryan Styles, Jamie, Rory, Lucy, Philip Normal, Squat, Delia Sparrow, the Actionettes, Richard Roberts and Rosemary, Tessa Clist, Emily Maben, Russel Martin, Lisa Jones, Kim Jenkins, Will Fowler, Charlie Phillips, Fiona from Banchory, Belle and Sebastian and every other band that has created the soundtrack to Tatty Devine.

IT ALL STARTED WITH...

a white leather wrist cuff, made from a snippet of an old belt and held together by a hairgrip...

Even before we met each other at art school, we'd always made things. We were the sort of girls who painted the scenery for school plays or backdrops for local bands, made our own hair scrunchies, and transformed rocks into ladybirds and bumblebees with enamel paint and sold them as doorstops in the summer holidays. At college we cut up our jeans and made them into skirts, fringed our T-shirts, made clothes from old patterns salvaged from charity shops and pretty much customised everything we went out in. And we needed a lot of looks for a lot of going out. We'd go and see bands and head out dancing and whatever we wore or made got ruined from high kicking on the bar, or rolling around on the floor of gig venues.

So we knew we wanted to keep on making stuff for a living, but we weren't exactly sure what – or how – to go about it.

A chance find of a mountain of leather sample books abandoned outside an upmarket furniture shop set us on the path that led to becoming Tatty Devine. Harriet found them on her way back from the pub, carted them home in the dead of night, and shoved them under her bed, where they languished for months. She had been wearing a leather cuff, sliced off a white lattice-work belt and held together with a hairclip, that had been getting lots of compliments. So, armed with craft knives and a lot of enthusiasm, we set about making some similar cuffs to sell. We cut up the sample books – they were a treasure trove of coloured leather, suede, snakeskin and ostrich skin in every shade of the rainbow – and abandoned the hairgrip clasp for a more secure fastening invented by Harriet's dad, Roger. And then we queued in the early hours to get a pitch on a market. On our first day out at Camden Market, a boy bought a cuff to put in a time capsule. It seemed like a lucky sign.

It was cold and damp on our stall – we had to make cardboard insoles for our shoes to keep our feet warm, and we dreamt of hot baths and glasses of whisky as the wind whistled around our ears – but mostly we just loved it. It was so exciting; you never knew who was going to walk up to the stall – stylists, boutique owners or friends, and people who would become friends and collaborators. We loved the camaraderie. At the end of the day we would do deals with other stallholders and get some brilliant stuff. Starting the business this way gave us the freedom to not get real jobs and remain outside the mainstream.

We learned to look at things in a different way. To tilt our heads to the side and see what happened.

We were hooked and wanted to make more and more. We made one-off designs from bits and pieces we found in charity shops, boot sales and markets. We transformed plectrums, cake decorations, dart flights and chess pieces into earrings and charm bracelets, necklaces and hair bobbles. The internet didn't really exist then (can you believe that?) so we sourced everything locally, using stuff that we found in shops or skips; instead of using Gumtree or eBay we took to the pavements, or to stationery shops and DIY emporiums. We were forced to be inventive. We popped our first collection in pink and white striped paper bags like old-fashioned pick'n'mix, and when we got our first fax machine (the height of technology at the time!) we felt-tipped the new number on to the bosoms of our T-shirts, took pictures, made finger puppets from the images and sent them out as our calling cards. There was no grand plan: it was all naïve, instinctive and, above all, fun.

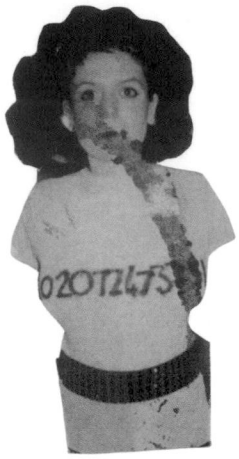

Rosie as a finger puppet. We made a load of us, all with different hairstyles.

A left-over token from Margate's defunct Dreamland, a favourite hang-out.

After getting a surprise order from a famous shop, we spent hot summer days gluing crystals on to belts, as forty tortoises mistook our varnished nails for cherry tomatoes in Rosie's east London garden. Another order was assembled in the front room, with our friends as a mini-production line, sewing big fake jewels on to belts and trying not to prick their fingers and bleed on to the white leather. We'd go to bed surrounded by the smell of contact adhesive and suede, and wake up bursting with ideas, learning new techniques and tricks as we went along.

We quickly realised that with some basic skills and a huge amount of imagination anyone can make original and stylish jewellery. As the years have gone by, we've moved from the huddle of our bedrooms and chilly market stalls to setting up a proper studio space and opening two shops. But we still feel exactly the way we did at the beginning. Nothing beats the amazing feeling of making something and heading out on the town with a brooch or a lovely new necklace inspired by a macramé owl discovered at a car boot sale, or simply wearing a little of what you fancy, strung together and made into something unique.

And that's what this book is all about. It's about getting to grips with some very basic jewellery-making techniques, and then letting your imagination run wild. There's not going to be anything here that's too tricky to understand, and it won't cost the earth in equipment and supplies. We'll explain how to make necklaces, leather cuffs, tape-measure rosettes and a whole jewellery box full of other accessories, using recycled and upcycled bits and bobs. We'll let you know what inspires us, share some Tatty Devine secrets, and give you the confidence to get making.

No training or big costs involved. Just good friends and a good eye.

Badges are always brilliant. Our friend Marc Pawson is the King!

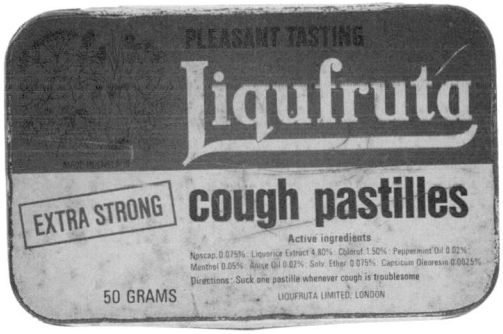

A lovely addition to our tin collection, the graphics are really beautiful.

Tools and findings

Although it's tempting to head out and buy loads of rainbow-coloured pliers, glue guns, drills and billions of findings and crystals, and then to stack them away in expensive plastic containers, it's nicer to make your own crafty corner with things you love.

When we started we stored our bits and pieces in lovely old cigar boxes collected by Rosie, first-aid tins and odd little boxes that we salvaged from charity shops. It was a treat to get them out when we were looking for a button or bead. The shelves in the Brick Lane studio were lined with recycled glass jars: we ate a lot of gherkins and some very choice pickles, and then we screwed the jars to the undersides of our shelves by their lids (we washed the jars out first). That way we could use the base of the shelves for storing even more jars and bits and bobs. Space has always been at a premium for us as we are terrific hoarders.

HOW TO MAKE GENIUS STORAGE

Pimp your shelf

You'll need:

- Empty jars
- Drill
- 2 mm drill bit
- Scrappy bit of wood
- Pencil
- Phillips screwdriver bit
- 2 screws per jar – (The screws must be shorter than the depth of the shelves)
- Cup hooks

Munch the contents of the jars, and then wash them out.

Unscrew the jar lids. Think about where you'd like them to go, and then draw around the lids on the underside of the shelves, using the pencil. Leave enough space between the jars so you can get your hand in to unscrew them.

On the inside of the jar lid, make two marks about 3 cm apart in the centre of the lid.

Lay the lid on a scrappy bit of wood and drill two holes right where your pencil marks are, using the 2 mm drill bit.

Hold the lid up to the circle you've drawn on the underside of the shelf, and poke the pencil through the holes you've just drilled. These dots are where the screws are going to go.

Now drill a tiny hole on to the pencil dots. Don't drill right through the shelf!

Swap the drill bit for a Phillips screwdriver bit and grab the screws. Hold the lid up to the pencilled circle, and push the screws into the tiny holes, give them a little twist so that they don't drop out when you're reaching for the drill.

Using the Phillips screwdriver bit, whoosh in the two screws. You need to have two screws or the jars will just spin round and round like a record and never undo!

Fill up the jars with all your bits and bobs and cool stuff and twist on to the lids.

Screwing cup hooks in between the jars is great too; you can hang work-in-progress necklaces on them, lengths of chain and dangly earrings, rulers, tape measures and key rings. They're also really handy if you need something to hook on when you're making a long plait or embarking on a piece of macramé.

$20
MILLICENT ZAHN
BOOK OF
Plastics Craft
HERBAL
Tetrosyl
Easy Spray
All Purpose Paint
ICI
Dulux
TRADE
Eggshell
Number 1
PLAYING CARDS

Rustins
CLEAR
DAN
SEMPER GELD
James VI of Scotland & his Queen
Assorted SCOTCH SHORTBREAD

TOOLS

The following pictures show you all the equipment you'll need to get started.

2 pairs of flat-nose pliers

Round-nose pliers

Wire cutters

A pair of hefty pliers

Hand-held hole punch

2 pairs of flat-nose pliers:
These are essential. You'll need them for opening jump rings (see page 24) and other bits of jewellery construction. Treat yourself, as these are the things that you'll use the most. But make sure you get smooth ones, not ones with ridges or teeth, as they mark the metal.

Round-nose pliers:
These are handy for curling wire. You can get ones with in-built wire cutters, which we like.

Wire cutters:
For snipping heavy wire and chain. You could use an old, rubbishy pair of scissors, but don't use your best pair as cutting wire will wreck the blades.

A pair of hefty pliers:
For tougher jobs. You can get ace ones at jumble sales, or car boot sales.

Hand-held hole punch:
The one on your office desk isn't going to be much help. Instead invest in a hand-held punch with a variety of hole sizes.

Tweezers

Set of Screwdrivers

Files

Hammer

Variety of drill bits

Tweezers:
For fiddly moments with tiny jump rings, fine chain or small crystals.

Set of screwdrivers:
For the doing and undoing of screws.

Files:
A small set of files come into their own for smoothing sharp bits or jagged edges.

Hammer:
For bashing things.

Hand drill or pendant drill:
Very useful, but they can be expensive. Borrow one from a DIY fiend, or go halves with a friend or partner in crime.

Variety of drill bits:
Invest in a selection of small drill bits: 0.8, 1.2, 1.8, 2, 2.5 and 3 mm are the sizes to go for.

Collets:
These hold tiny drill bits in place snugly in the drill.

Stanley knife/ Craft knife/Scalpel | *Hacksaw* | *Needlework scissors* | *Pinking shears* | *Scribe and bradawl* | *Soft brush* | *Paintbrushes*

Stanley knife/Craft knife/ Scalpel:
All of these cut with a lovely clean line. Remember to stock up on spare super-sharp blades.

Hacksaw:
This little saw will make light work of stuff that defeats the wire cutters.

Scissors:
You really need a few pairs, such as paper scissors, fabric scissors, pinking shears, an all-rounder pair (for rough-and-ready jobs) and an elegant pair of needlework scissors for intricate jobs. Our favourites are bird-shaped.

Scribe and bradawl:
Handy for marking, scoring and scuffing the surfaces of things that are going to be glued. And for bashing a pilot hole.

A soft brush:
Lovely for brushing away dust and debris and the final bit of sprucing up on a make.

Paintbrushes:
A selection is a good thing. Use them for painting, staining, gluing and varnishing. Always clean out your brushes properly.

Thimble *Knitting needles* *Pins* *Tape measure* *2-part epoxy glue* *Superglue* *Contact adhesive* *Glue gun*

Thimble:
Sewing leather and heavy fabric can be tough, so a thimble will protect your fingers.

Knitting needles:
A small knitting needle is great if you need to poke something, or if you want to get busy with the glue but your object is small and you're all fingers and thumbs.

Pins:
Handy for poking and pinning.

Tape measure:
For measuring longer things like ribbons and chains.

Glue:
2-part epoxy, we love Araldite, superglue, contact adhesive and glue gun.

Bead threading needle

Needles

Cotton buds

Cocktail sticks

Paint

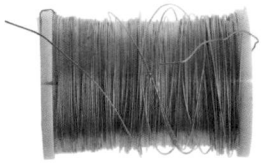

Jewellery wire and thicker wire

Beeswax

Blu-Tack

Other handy things for your storage shelves:

Wet and dry sandpaper
Danish oil
White spirit
Varnish
Spray paint
Dust mask
Eye protectors
Masking tape
Rubber mallet
Metal ruler
Cutting mat

Beads and bits:

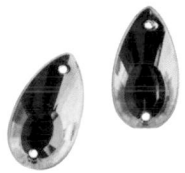

Sew-on gems

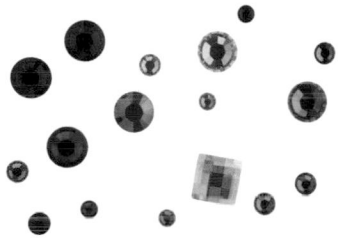

Flat-back crystals

Seed beads

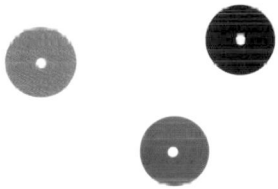

Sequins

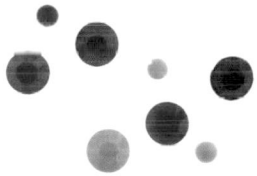

Plastic stick-on gems

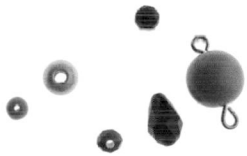

Beads

Bits and pieces

Charms

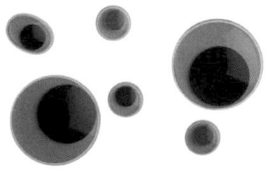

Googly eyes

FINDINGS

Jewellery is all about joining different bits of things together, and these bits and pieces will help you do just that.

Jump rings are indispensable. They are a simple loop of wire, with a split at the top that's opened with pliers (see page 18). You can connect chains to them, dangle trinkets from them and attach a necklace clasp to them. They come in a variety of sizes and different sorts of metals so it's a good idea to play around with them and find out what works best. You want a jump ring that's strong enough for your chosen make, as flimsy ones will come apart and all your hard work will be undone, and you want one that's the right size – discreet is the way to go for delicate jewellery, but go large for chunky looks. Ideally you want the jump ring to move freely on whatever you're making, so experiment with different sizes until it feels and looks just right.

Here are our favourites:

Tiny jump rings (3mm) work brilliantly with fine chain. We love the ones that are slightly oval-shaped, with the split along the long edge.

Small jump rings (4mm) They're handy to have around for more delicate projects.

Regular jump rings (6mm) are used for attaching trinkets, charms and necklace clasps. They're strong enough to link strands of heavier chain and chunky beads, and are just right to act as an end ring on a necklace.

Large jump rings (12mm) are great with bigger charms or heavy chains.

Bolt clasps
have a tiny spring inside – you push back the little lever, and the spring opens the clasp; which is why it's also known as a spring clasp.

Lobster clasps
look just like crustacean claws, and are a fine fastener for a bracelet or necklace. Check that they open and close well, as occasionally the catch can be a little sticky.

A head pin
is like a full stop. It's a length of wire with a disc soldered on one end. Head pins are also used to attach beads to each other, or to the necklace or bracelet chain.

Eye pins
are pieces of wire with a loop on one end that are brilliant for linking beads and charms. They come in a variety of lengths, but you can easily snip them with a wire cutter or you can make your own with fine wire and some round-nose pliers.

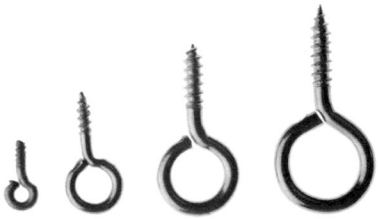

Screw-in eyelets
are found in the DIY shop, and are great for putting up net curtains. But you can also screw them into heavy objects, pop on a jump ring and attach them to the chain of your choice.

Chains
come in all shapes and sizes. You can re-use old necklaces, recycle junk shop finds or buy new chain from craft shops and online. They come in a variety of types and colours, with odd but lovely names such as silver rhodium, gilt, burnished gold and hematite. Here are our favourites:

Curb chains

Trace chains

Belcher chain

Ball chain

Sam Browne studs
were invented in World War Two by a certain Sam Browne, who turned a bullet into a nifty way of fastening together pieces of leather or heavy-duty fabric belts and cuffs. It's known as a 'bibble' in Tattyworld.

Callotes
are used with crimps, and are threaded onto the end of strings of beads; their loop lets you attach the string of beads to jump rings and clasps.

Crimp beads
are used for finishing ends on strings of beads, and work just like a knot. They are little tubes that are squashed flat with the pliers to form a tight seal to stop the beads from sliding off.

Bead caps
are little domes of metal that can be added on to strings of beads or stuck on top of beads or round objects to turn them into a necklace, with the help of a jump ring.

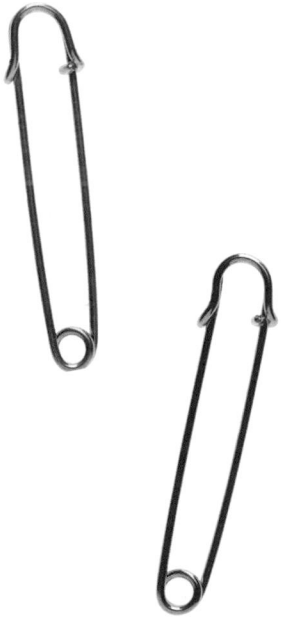

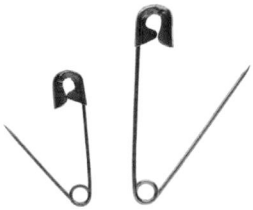

Kilt pins and safety pins
are great for displaying charms and rosettes on. They come in lots of different sizes, and some even have soldered rings so you can give your trinkets more space. Remember to adorn the bar of the pin that doesn't open, otherwise you won't be able to fasten your new accessory to your lapel.

Beading silks
come in lovely colours and different thicknesses and lengths. Some even have the beading needle already attached! Always choose one that's thin enough to thread through the hole on the bead.

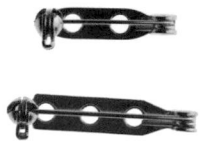

Brooch backs
are the simplest way of transforming a lovely trinket into a piece of jewellery. Check the hinge and clasp of the brooch back to make sure it works before getting busy with the glue.

Cufflinks
are lovely and old-fashioned, but you can give them an up-to-date look by gluing small, cool, flat things to the flat disc of this finding.

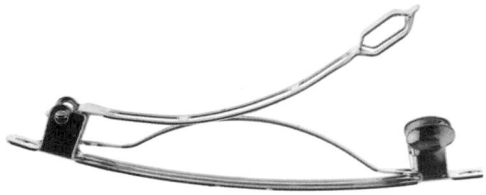

A barrette
is a great base for creating some snazzy hair accessories. Use a glue gun to fix your decoration on to it. Sewing or wiring on stuff will work a treat as well.

Ring shanks
are, unsurprisingly, necessary to make rings. The ones with the flat discs are perfect for sticking on interesting flat things; the ones with the soldered-on jump rings are great for adding on charms or beads. Most come with an adjustable band, which is perfect if you're making the rings as presents.

Studs
give you options. If you're aiming for gluing something quite large and flat into an earring, go for studs with a soldered-on disc. Bumpy shapes and little things work best with a drilled in post. If you're allergy-prone, splash out on solid silver earring posts; it's no fun having dashing earrings but itchy ears.

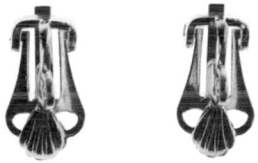

Clip-ons
And there are always clip-ons if your ears aren't pierced.

Fish hooks
are what you use if you want an earring that dangles. They have a handy small loop, ready for you to attach your chosen object.

In the mood for making

Before you start making it's nice to have a clean and orderly space in which to work, with good light, a comfy chair and a sketchbook to scribble out your ideas.

And it's a good idea to pop a notebook in your bag too, as you never know when inspiration will strike. Here are some of the things that make us think:

Old stuff; tatty things that are tarnished, used and well-loved; charity shops, jumble sales, car boots, flea markets, skips, street finds; old books; National Trust buildings; music and records; pop culture; old magazines, like the *Golden Hands* craft periodicals and the vintage *Vogues*, beautifully bound by Harriet's nan; Rosie's granny's sewing and gardening books, which she wrote and self-published.

Plastic seventies bangles; old children's story books; Letterpress; pin badges; kitsch ceramics; anything giant or miniature; collections of things: postcards, stamps, letters, slides; silk scarves; old watches; old spectacles; world globes; collapsible toys; enamel badges; fans; popper beads...

We love the fact that one girl's rubbish is another girl's treasure.

Bacon's LARGE SCALE Map of the Isle of Wight
FREE with any DEVELOPING & PRINTING ORDER VALUE 22.OR OVER
THE RUBBISHMEN OF SOHO
GIN
GIN
VOLUME
LIFE WORLD LIBRARY
THE UNITED STATES
RE-JOICE RE-JOICE
INDIETRACKS
an indiepop festival
2009
REALM
Special Pattern
GEORGE AND DRAGO
Taylor's
WATERPROOF FILMS DRESSINGS
FULL PROTECTION AGAINST
WATER, GREASE and OIL
The POPPYE and Friends Knitting Book
Tatty Devine
28b Brick Lane
London
E2 7EB
The Zoo
Isabel Campbell
Fashion Hair Accessory
DOUBLE HEADER
STEAM ROLLERS vs SUFFRA JETS
LONDON ROLLERGIRLS PRESENTS
GRAND SLAM!
1ST SEASON CHAMPIONSHIP
THE FACE
Oasis
Electrelane
TWO FOR JOY
ANIMALS
ALAN JAMES
People at work
THE SAILOR
THE COMPLETE COUNTRY BIKE BOOK
Happy
Charms
TATTY DEVINE

Whenever your heart guides your hand
Funeral Director
At the Hour of Need
Funeral Home
Funeral Home
Mon Journal
Thrift SCORE
The Zine About Thrifting · Issue 8
ANTHROPOLOGY A GO GO
NEW WORK BY
Figanovsky
ISLINGTON ARTS FACTORY
MANRESA ROAD SW3
PARTY LINE
Bicentennial '20th
DIANE ARBUS
FOOD ORDER
FOUR ORDER NUMBER
ORDNANCE SURVEY.
ISLE OF WIGHT.
PRICE ONE SHILLING & SIXPENCE
SUSANNA
SAVAGE MESSIAH
SAVAGE MESSIAH
RIVER WALBROOK
THE SPECIALS
2 TONE
Ghost Town
Why?
Friday Night Saturday Morning
Come and Celebrate with us.
SDAY 1st OCTOBER. 6.30-8.30
5 COLUMBIA RD, LONDON E2.
BLACK AND WHITE!
Tatty Devine

Chicks on Speed
riot grrl
CRAZY HORSE
TYPICAL GIRLS? THE STORY OF THE SLITS
HAIRSPRAY
ALL TOMORROW'S PARTIES
SONIC YOUTH SUPER FURRY ANIMALS
MOGWAI STEREOLAB
SUPER MEND
BOW WOW WOW
"I Want Candy"
Bette Davis and Joan Crawford
WHAT EVER HAPPENED TO BABY JANE?
ALL ABOUT MY MOTHER
a film by ALMODOVAR
SUBCULTURE
HEBDIGE
STEREOHTOTAL
MARK PAWSON
NOGGINS+
POP CORN
SILLY THING
Sex Pistols
Fresh Crisp!
the B-52
Goldy Peaches
The Duke Spirit

Age 3-6
fuzzy felt shapes
140 pieces
BBC
Ashley Blues
Fashion
15
CHEAP Date
for thinkin
MARKETS OF LONDON
ABCDEFGHI
JKLMNOPQR
STUVWXYZ
abcde
lmnopqrst
vwxyz!.
Grip/Strip
WEAR MORE BADGES
pop machine
I love you
THE NEW
SOHO SHOP IS NOW
OPEN
Brewer St London W1F 9UL 0207 433 2257
THE EEL
NEW SHOP
HAND SHADOWS
SECOND SERIES
IRON ON
WADDINGTON'S
SHAPED
JIG MAP
WITH PLACE-NAME QUIZ
MADE IN GREAT BRITAIN BY
PANTONE
40
formula guide
coated/uncoated
MARK FAWSON
DISINFOTAINMENT

First things first

A length of chain, a clasp and a few jump rings can be transformed into a dainty decoration or a necklace that sweeps the floor.

There are thick chains, thin chains and medium chains, and the sizes of jump rings and lobster clasps vary too. As a rule of thumb, the thicker the chain the bigger the jump rings and the lobster clasps. The jump ring should comfortably fit the chain, with a bit of wiggle room. You might have to try out different-sized jump rings to get a good fit.

Here's how the different sizes of jump ring can connect to different thicknesses of chain...

Tatty's Top 5 'Chain Songs'

'Chain of Fools'
Aretha Franklin

'Chain Reaction'
Diana Ross

'Chain Gang'
Sam Cooke

'The Chain'
Fleetwood Mac

'Chainsaw'
The Ramones

SKIN

HOW TO MAKE A BASIC NECKLACE

Cha cha chain

You'll need:

- A length of fine chain
- Ruler
- Wire cutters, or an old pair of scissors
- 2 tiny jump rings
- 2 pairs of flat-nose pliers
- 2 small jump rings
- 1 lobster clasp

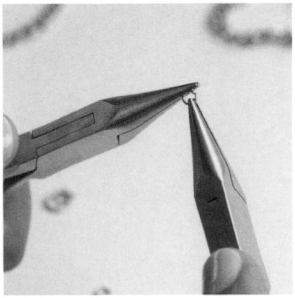

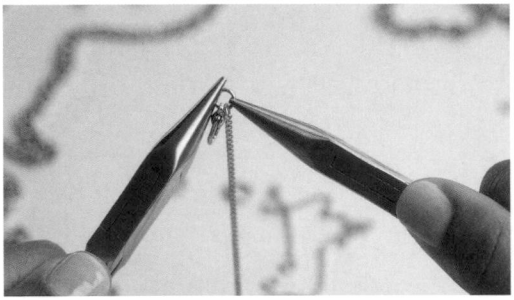

If you're making a short necklace you'll need approx. 40 cm of chain, for a medium necklace about 60 cm and for a longish necklace your measurement is about 80 cm.

Measure your chain with a ruler and then cut with the wire cutters. You could use an old pair of scissors, but don't use your best ones, as cutting chain will play havoc with the sharpness of the blades.

Open the tiny jump rings with the pliers. To do this, grasp one tiny jump ring in one of the pairs of pliers, with the split in the jump ring facing upwards. Grab the second pair of pliers in the other hand, at right angles to the first pair, and use it to twist the jump ring apart at the split.

A quarter turn towards you should do the trick. Don't go too far, and don't be too brutal. Carefully attach one end of the chain to your open jump ring and then close the jump ring.

Open the small jump ring using the method above, and pop on the tiny jump ring on the end of the chain. Close the jump ring.

Do the same on the other end of the chain: attach the remaining tiny jump ring, then attach the remaining small jump ring to it and pop on the lobster clasp. Close the small jump ring.

If you want to make a bracelet, do the same wire cutters/pliers/lobster clasp/jump rings thing, but use approx. 18 cm of chain. You might need larger jump rings with thicker chain.

Top Tatty Tip

With some thick chains you can open the links with pliers, rather than snipping them with the wire cutter. With a really fat chain, get out the hacksaw.

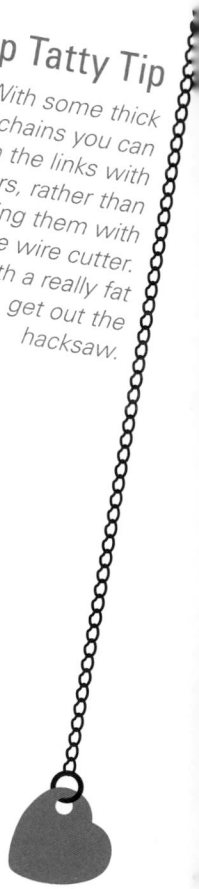

LEADERS

To make your necklace adjustable in length you can add a leader. The easiest way to make a leader is to attach a length of medium trace chain to the non-clasp end of the necklace.

A tiny toy spanner saved from a Christmas cracker. Anything miniature is great!

Open the non-clasp end of the small jump ring with pliers, slide a short length of trace chain on to the jump ring, and then close the jump ring.

Make sure your lobster clasp is a good fit with the medium trace chain (see above), so that it's easy to do and undo anywhere along the length of the leader.

You can also pop a regular-sized jump ring in at any point along the length of your chain, for dramatically different ways of wearing the necklace (see above).

Cut the chain with the wire cutter and then link it to a regular jump ring you can attach the clasp to. If your chain is too fine, add a small or tiny jump ring to both the cut ends of the chain.

When you come to do up your necklace, you can fasten the lobster clasp to the ring at the end of the necklace, or to the jump ring in the middle of the chain. And you can add a series of regular jump rings on the length of the chain for even more variety. Or you could get really fancy and use beads instead of chain to separate the jump rings (see p 111).

HOW TO MAKE A BOW TIE NECKLACE

It's a kind of magic

Vintage shops are full of beautiful dresses. But they are also full of odd little things that you might like the look of, but aren't sure exactly how to go about wearing: nylons that won't stretch enough to fit an actual leg into, but come in pretty packets, and lovely old-fashioned bow ties that are designed to clip to the sort of old-fashioned dress shirts that aren't made any more. Harriet's granddad was a magician: he swallowed razor blades, and then pulled them out of his mouth on a length of string. He always wore a bow tie. You too can add a dash of magic to your outfit with this Bow Tie Necklace. It's as easy as *hey presto* ... but without the danger of slicing your tongue in half.

You'll need:

- 1 short 40 cm chain necklace (see page 36)
- Wire cutters
- 2 small jump rings
- 2 pairs of flat-nose pliers
- 1 vintage or charity shop bow tie (with the metal bit on the back.)

Optional extras:

- 1 regular jump ring
- 2 beads, one big, one small
- 1 eye pin
- 1 head pin
- 1 pair of round-nose pliers

Make up your necklace using the method shown earlier.

Hold the necklace by the clasp and cut it in half with the wire cutters, opposite the clasp.

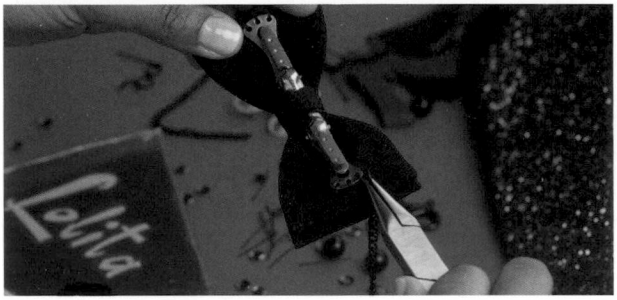

Attach a small jump ring to each side of the cut ends of the necklace, using the flat-nose pliers.

Attach the chain to the holes in the back of the bow tie. The jump rings go through the bow tie holes, and the pliers neatly close the jump rings. (If your chain is finer, attach tiny jump rings to each end of the chain, and then attach the small jump rings.)

If you're feeling fancy, you can make it adjustable. With the addition of a regular jump ring your bowtie necklace can go from skimming your chest to nestling at the collar of your shirt. At the non-clasp end of the necklace, 70 mm in, pop in a jump ring, using the wire cutters and pliers technique (see page 36).

You can also add a couple of beads for a decorative flourish, as befits a magician. On the bigger bead, thread on an eye pin. Trim the wire, with the wire cutters, so that there's about 10 mm sticking out. Then bend the wire down at a right angle with the pliers. The next bit is a little fiddly, but you'll soon get going with a bit of practice. With the round-nose pliers, roll the wire up into a loop, with tiny twists, rolling away from you. Try to get it to roughly the same size as the loop at the other end. Then, holding each loop with the flat-nose pliers, check that both loops are facing in the same direction. Tweak gently if they aren't.

On the smaller bead, thread on the head pin. Trim the wire and do the loop thing again. Join the beads together through the loops; the small bead is the full stop. Then you can attach them to the non-clasp end of the necklace.

Top TATTY Tip

If the bow tie doesn't have the appropriate hardware on the back, sew two small jump rings to the top corners of the bow tie.

Make sure you've flipped the bow tie over, so you're working on the back. If you sew them about 10 mm in from the top and side edges, they'll be invisible from the front.

Magic.

HOW TO MAKE A LEATHER CUFF

Channel your inner '80s pop star

When we first started out, we had to create our jewellery in our bedrooms and odd little corners of our flats. Eventually we decided to get a small studio, and went for a long stroll in East London looking for a space. It didn't look too promising until we sat on a wall for a rest at the top of Brick Lane. Opposite us, in the summer sunshine, there was a boarded-up shop. It was a wreck inside, with rubbish up to our knees, but it had beautiful red-stained glass, and we fell in love with it. We gutted the shop with the help of Harriet's dad, and we moved in with all our equipment – a cutting board, a Stanley knife and a metal ruler. And that's basically all the stuff you'll need to make this lovely leather cuff.

Make an arrow-headed paper template, using the shape pictured opposite. A good standard fit is about 200 mm in length, but if you have very small or big wrists you'll probably need to play around with the sizing. Add or decrease the length by cutting the template in half and adding in or removing paper to the middle of the strip to make it bigger or smaller, and getting busy with the sticky tape.

Trace the shape of your freshly made paper template on to the leather, with the scribe or the old biro. Trace the slit too.

You'll need:

- Paper
- Pencil
- Scissors
- Sticky tape
- Length of leather or pleather (the cuff works best with leather that's about 2 mm thick)
- A scribe, or something to mark the surface of the leather (a biro that's run out of ink would do the trick)
- Cutting mat or board
- Metal ruler
- Sharp craft knife
- Hand-held hole punch

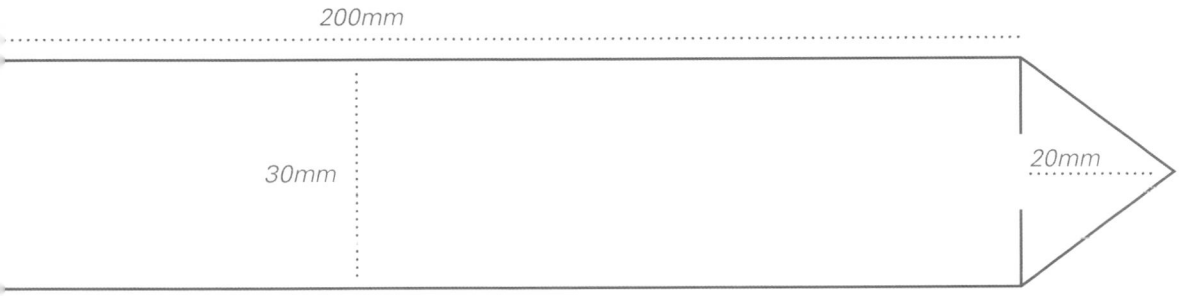

Put the leather on the cutting board, and use the edge of the metal ruler to cut out the shape with the sharp craft knife. BE CAREFUL, don't cut off your fingers!

It might take a few swipes of the knife to get through the leather surface, but aim for nice clean lines, and make sure you've cut right through the leather to avoid hirsute edges.

Use the hole punch and punch 2 mm holes at each end of the traced slit. Then cut the slit. The first few times you try and pull the arrow head through the slit it might be a bit stiff, but over time the leather will soften, and it'll get easier to fasten.

Oh, and on some leathers the colour is not dyed right through, leaving unsightly edges when you make your cuts. You could use specialised dye to stain the edges, but a steady hand and a marker pen would work too.

How you can customise your cuff:

Let your imagination go to town decorating your cuffs. We like brogue detailing and sewing chain down the edges.

HOW TO MAKE A GEM HAIR BAND

Bobby Dazzler

Rosie used to have a part-time job in a vintage shop called Steinberg and Tolkien on the King's Road, and liked to dress the part. One Friday she was sporting a big, bold, gem-studded hair band, when it was spotted by a *Vogue* stylist who was in the shop supposedly browsing for olden-days looks, but who instead fell in love with Rosie's thoroughly modern bright pink hair accessory. She immediately asked to see the Tatty collection. Harriet's mum got straight in her car with her sewing machine (because ours was a bit worse for wear) and we spent the whole weekend sewing gems onto leather, and headed to the *Vogue* office on Monday. Before we knew it Erin O'Connor was wearing a Tatty Devine cuff in *Vogue*'s millennium issue. It was a mad time, but brilliant.

We love anything that says "Paris". Especially if it's shiny.

You'll need:

- Some lush soft leather, approx. 300 x 50 mm
- Craft knife
- 2 rulers (one metal), or anything with a straight edge
- Cutting mat or board
- Masking tape
- Araldite glue (see page 54)
- Old flyer or playing card
- Cocktail stick
- A lovely selection of snazzy sew-on multi-coloured plastic gems
- Leather sewing needle
- Buttonhole thread (in a matching or clashing colour) and thimble
- Needlework scissors
- Pigskin/suede to use as a backing, approx. 310 x 60 mm

Contact adhesive

Scrap of old cardboard

Brand-new, fearsomely sharp craft knife blade

Hand-held hole punch

2 lengths of ribbon
about 80 cm long; grosgrain or velvet are the best (satin is too slippy and slidey to stay put in your hair)

Optional extras:

Rubber mallet

Scribe

Round coin (to draw round)

Bra slider

Elastic

Think what you want your hair band to look like. You could go crazy with the crystals – haphazard and mad looks fun – or you can take the careful approach, and work out a beautifully decorous design.

Start by cutting a strip of leather, approximately 300 mm by 50 mm (or any size of your choice), using your craft knife, a metal ruler and the cutting board.

If you're going for the crazy gem approach, place the two rulers on either side of the leather strip, 5 mm in from the long sides. Make sure they are straight and parallel, then hold them steady with a bit of masking tape.

Mix up some Araldite on a flyer or playing card using a cocktail stick. Leaving 30 mm at each end, stick on as many gems as you can cram in between the two rulers. Use the cocktail stick to help position them precisely.

If order is your thing, mix up some Araldite on a flyer or playing card and line the gems up 5 mm from the bottom of the leather, and 30 mm in from the left-hand side. Stick the gems on all the way up the strip but call a halt 30 mm from the other end. Your ribbon will go on here a little later.

Remember to glue your gems with the holes running in a straight line along the length of the band, or your stitching will be all over the shop!

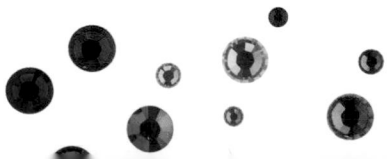

This cute spinning top was a present from our artist friend Mark Pawson

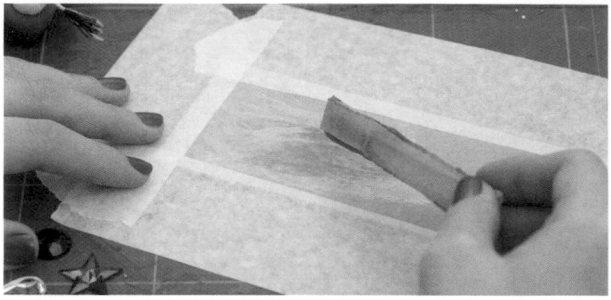

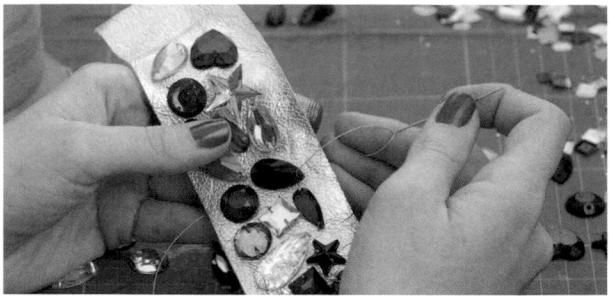

Wait until the glue is dry. Then start a-sewing the gems on to the leather, using the leather needle, thimble, and the buttonhole thread. Try and match the colour of your thread to the colour of your leather, unless you want to make a deliberate contrast statement.

Snip untidy threads with the elegant needlework scissors. It's also worth double-checking that all the gems are sewn securely through all the holes.

The next step is to make a backing to cover up all your careful stitches. Cut the suede 5 mm bigger than the leather, so that's about 310 mm by 60 mm. Stick the suede strip to the cutting board, right-side down, with the masking tape. You can get away with putting a strip of masking tape only on the top and bottom of the suede, but it's best to stick down the sides too. Make sure the suede is taut before you stick it.

Slather the back of the suede with a thin coat of contact adhesive, carefully spreading it on with a bit of old card. Leave no bit uncoated.

Make sure you open a window, or better still, do it outside as the glue is pretty smelly.

Cover the back of the gemmed leather with glue too, making sure it reaches all the way to the edges. Wait for the glue to become dry to the touch – the packet will tell you how long that's going to take.

You may as well get the glue off your fingers while you're whistling and waiting, then there'll be no bad crime-scene gluey prints on the good side of the leather.

Really stubborn bits of glue demand white spirit, but warm water and soap generally works, as does facial scrub.

Then join the backs of the suede and the leather together, and press down firmly. Bang it gently with a rubber mallet if you happen to have one about.

Change the blade in the craft knife to a brand-new super-sharp one. This is essential, as one false move and all your hard work will go to wrack and ruin. No pressure then.

Align the metal ruler up against the gems and cut through the leather, as close to the gems as possible, but without cutting any of the stitches, on both the long sides.

Then cut across the ends. For a fancy finish you could round off the corners; this looks especially nice on wide leather bands. A good pair of scissors is just the thing to give you a nice clean edge.

To make a curve guideline, use a scribe and a coin on the reverse before cutting. Punch a 4 mm hole about 10 mm in from the edge of each end of the headband.

Next up is the ribbon. Fold one piece of ribbon in half, and put the fold through one of the holes at the end of the leather band. Thread the ends of the ribbon through the loop you've just made. Pull the tail of the ribbon to tighten the knot.

Do like you just did with the other piece of ribbon, and the hole at the other end of the hair band. Around 80 mm of ribbon on each side will neatly tie your hair band on, but there's nothing to stop you having a cascade of multi-coloured ribbons sweeping to the floor.

And ribbon isn't the only way to finish off the hair band: leather or a bra-slider-and-elastic combo work too.

For the bra-slider option

First, grab a bra and check how the slider works. You're going to be doing exactly the same with the hair band. Sew the slider to one end of the 10mm elastic through the middle bar. Thread the other end of the elastic through the hole in the hair band, from back to front, then thread it back through the slider so the slider moves freely along the length of the elastic. This loop is what makes the hair band adjustable. Finally, thread the other end of the elastic through the other hole in the hair band and sew securely in place.

For the leather option

Assuming you have enough leather left, cut two strips about 10 mm wide and 500 mm long. Tie a knot close to the end of each piece of leather, and thread one into each hole of the head band, with the knot on the inside.

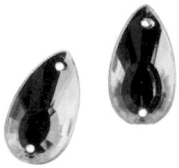

HOW TO MAKE A PHOTOCOPY WATCH BRACELET

Tick tock, we can't stop

It doesn't have to be a watch, but this was one of the first things we laminated. Back then we kept loads of scrap books with all kinds of pictures, and photo albums with pages and pages of interesting snaps, as it was tricky to find images. Nowadays there's tons of copyright-free stuff on the net, and inspiring images available at a click of the mouse on sites like tumblr, so you won't be stuck for ideas.

You could go for a diamond bracelet, or a giant stick of chewing gum, or if you have something very precious or sentimental to you, that you'd be broken-hearted to lose, you could make a laminate of that, and wear it without fear. Anything will work, but the basic dimensions are about 300 mm by 200 mm.

You'll need:

- 1 picture of a watch with a strap
- Digital camera or scanner
- Photo editing software, if you want to play around with your pic
- Computer
- Printer
- Paper
- Local stationer with an A4 laminating machine
- Scissors
- A piece of self adhesive Velcro

Top TATTY Tip

Go wild with the lamination. Collect seed packets and turn your necklace into an allotment. Or make a memento charm bracelet, using reduced-size holiday photographs and the faces of your friends.

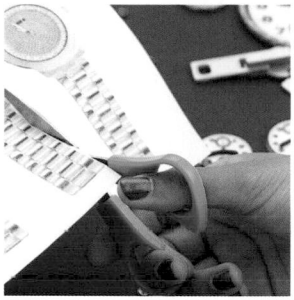

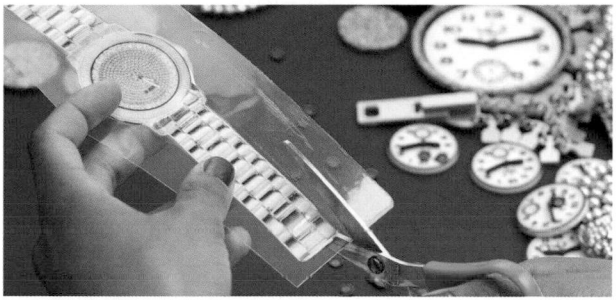

First pick an image of a watch. It can come from a magazine, or be the real thing.

Take a photo of it. Make sure you shoot it directly from above so that there's no distortion. Or you can scan it instead.

Upload the photo to your computer, and adjust the image to life size.

Have some fun by zooming in and changing the maker's mark to your name, and the date to a special date – your birthday, a party date, a date date.

Print it out, cut it out and try it on. If you're happy, then hurray. If not, edit the image on screen and reprint. Make a few more, enough to fill up a sheet of A4.

Sashay down to the stationers with your cut-outs. Make sure they stay flat.

Pop the images in between the layers of laminate, leaving a 4 mm gap around each one.

Let the machine do its thing. Head home at top speed and get busy with the scissors.

Carefully cut out your images, 2 mm from their edges, so that the paper stays snugly sealed between the laminate.

On the strap end of the watch, stick a 20 mm x 20 mm piece of sticky Velcro to the top end. Try it on, to work out where to stick the matching piece of Velcro on the back of the buckle end. When you're pleased with its position, get sticking.

Rosie discovered this beautiful broken watch on a market stall: it's right twice a day.

Araldite
Araldite

Sticky stuff

Here's the Tatty Devine guide to getting stuck in.

We loved PVA glue at school – it worked brilliantly with glitter, it stuck paper dolls' house furniture together, and made the best fake skin (coat both hands with a big splurge of PVA, wait for it to dry, and then carefully, carefully, carefully peel it off). A DIY horror-film moment. You can have just as much fun with more grown-up glue: dab it to the back of your favourite trinkets, add a brooch back or an earring post and you've made a piece of statement jewellery.

♣ Here's a small but important fact: grease repels glue. Chances are that any charity shop find or car boot discovery may well be a bit worse for wear on the dirt front. Luckily a spot of cleaning will sort that out. Warm soapy water is perfect for non-porous materials like glass, plastic, metal and crystals. When everything looks spick and span wipe the area that's going to be glued with white spirit, as this'll get rid of any traces of grease that may have been left behind.

♦ Glue also likes a bit of rough. For the glue to do its sticky best it needs a surface with a bit of texture, so on smooth, shiny surfaces get rubbing with a coarse-grade sandpaper, or use a sharp bradawl on the bit that's going to be covered in glue. The official name for this is 'keying'.

♦ It's a good idea to cover your work surface with old newspaper, as it makes tidying up much easier, and have an old rag or some tissues to hand in case of mishaps. In the case of fast-drying glue, assemble everything you need before you start sticking, and there won't be an *'OH NOOOOOOO!'* moment followed by a scene of you dashing madly around the room looking for that missing something.

♥ Always glue on a level surface, otherwise things could start slipping and sliding as they dry and when you return to your brooch its back might be awry, and not in a good way. If your treasure isn't flat, prop it up with a nugget of Blu-Tack; that'll level things off nicely.

♣ Even though strong glue will stick most things together, there are exceptions. It's all to do with physics, leverage and force. So even the strongest bond won't keep a ruler stuck to a ring back. Oh science, you are so important.

♦ Things can get a bit messy, with stray fingerprints and glue trails on your finished piece. Cotton buds, a soft cloth, white spirit and elbow grease will work on non-porous surfaces. If there are huge lumps of glue you'll need a scalpel or a knife to clean them off. Glue marks on wood can be sanded off, but sometimes the glue will soak into the grain and leave a mark. And be warned: removing glue from suede is nigh on impossible.

♠ Oh and glue can be a bit smelly, so try to make sure you have some fresh air coming into your workspace. And breathe. *Ahhhhh.*

A Word on Araldite

We love Araldite. It is a two-part epoxy resin glue, and it is genius; it's probably the most useful glue when it comes to costume jewellery. It sticks most things and it's strong, but there are a few things to bear in mind before you get to work.

First up, always read the instructions. Boring, but essential. Then, always squeeze the exact same amounts out of both tubes. Unless the mix is 50/50 it will NEVER dry. *Never.* Not ever.

Next, it's really important to mix it properly. Our maxim is: 'When you think you've mixed it enough – mix it a bit more.' Especially the bits of glue that skulk on the edges – make sure they're part of the party. Our tools for this job? A handy cocktail stick and some old flyers or playing cards. Harriet's brother was also a magician and one of his specialities was swallowing playing cards: he would spit them back out at us when we were trying to make jewellery. The floor and the ceiling were littered with odd jacks and kings and queens, but they were very handy for mixing batches of glue on.

Always make sure you mix enough glue for the job that needs doing, but not too much at once as you only have a few minutes of maximum freshness. So if you are planning on covering your shoes in hundreds of crystals, then mix the glue in small batches on a fresh piece of card, using a fresh cocktail stick each time.

The final tip is the trickiest one: WAIT UNTIL THE GLUE IS DRY. Tempting as it is to wear your new make straight away, try and be patient. That way, you and your new jewellery will have a lasting relationship, rather than coming unstuck immediately. Leave it to dry overnight, if you can.

This was once a teddy bear nose. Our friend Rocky knew we'd love it.

HOW TO MAKE A RADIO BROOCH

Radio days and disco nights

We love Dansettes and transistor radios, and mini musical instruments. We like the way they look, especially if they are red and plastic, but they also remind us how important music is to us. We've always made mix tapes, bought records and CDs and headed off to see our favourite bands play live. Nothing beats turning the dial and hearing the Shangri-Las over the airwaves.

You'll need:

Small plastic radio, or any other cute, flat, plastic item that takes your fancy

Bradawl

Araldite (see opposite)

Old flyer or playing card

Cocktail stick

Brooch back

Top TATTY Tip

Have you ever lost a brooch when dancing just a little bit too much at a gig or a club? Annoying, very annoying. Here's an easy way to stop that happening ever again. Do up your brooch, and then squish a bit of Blu-Tack all around the clasp. Now it won't come undone under even the most dramatic dance-floor duress.

The green lion is another ace find from a boot fair rummage box.

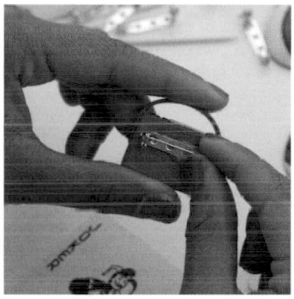

Before you start, decide where you want the brooch back to go. It's a good idea to stick it towards the top of your trinket, as that way your finished brooch will nestle nicely against your jumper, without sagging. If you have a fondness for wearing your brooches on your left-hand side, glue the brooch back with the hinge facing right, as this makes it easier to do it up and undo it. If you favour the right, glue the back with the hinge facing left. And if you're sticking the brooch back on vertically, put the hinge at the top, so if the clasp does come undone your brooch will (hopefully) stay pinned to the fabric in time for you to notice.

Clean and key the area on the back of the radio that you're going to glue with the bradawl (see page 53).

Mix up the Araldite on a flyer or playing card, according to the instructions, using a cocktail stick – and don't forget the Tatty maxim (see left).

Slather the Araldite generously to the reverse of the brooch back with the cocktail stick and then stick the brooch back to the reverse of the little radio.

Leave it to dry.

HOW TO MAKE A GLASS STOPPER PENDANT

Heart of glass

In a box full of curious smashed glasses and bottle pieces on a stall at Bridport market we came across this perfect glass stopper. We're not sure what it came from – a scent bottle, or a vial to store tears – but it was perfect for a pendant.

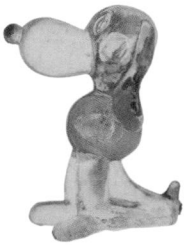

We couldn't resist this perky plastic dog. He's just waiting to be made into something cool.

You'll need:

- 1 head pin
- 1 bead cup
- 2 pairs of flat-nose pliers
- 1 pair of round-nose pliers
- 1 glass stopper
  or other rounded tricket
- Cup of uncooked rice or couscous
- Araldite (see page 54)
- Old flyers or playing cards
- Cocktail stick
- Cotton bud
- White spirit
- 1 regular jump ring
- 1 chain necklace (see page 36)

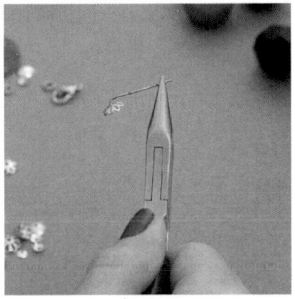

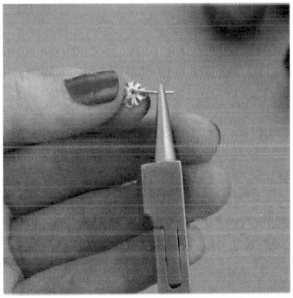

We were obsessed by jacks at school, we played every single break time.

Sometimes sticking round or unusual shapes down with some Blu-Tack works fine but you can also bed your chosen object in a bowl of rice or couscous to keep it level. That will leave both hands free for gluing. Best not to eat the rice afterwards though.

Firstly, thread the head pin through the bead cup and trim it to 10mm. With some flat-nose pliers bend the head pin down at a right angle. The next bit is tricky, but you'll soon get the hang of it. With the round-nose pliers roll the wire of the head pin into a loop, by making tiny twists rolling away from you.

Place the bead cup on top of your glass stopper (or another rounded trinket of your choice). Adjust with the pliers for a snug fit. Remove the bead cup again.

Plop the glass stopper into the rice, making sure it's nice and level.

Mix up the Araldite on a flyer or playing card and splodge it generously inside the bead cup with a cocktail stick. Then pop the gluey bead cup back on to the glass stopper, wiping off any glue that squishes out with a cotton bud. Leave it to dry.

Clean off any glue trails with white spirit, using a cotton bud.

Open the regular jump ring with the pliers, attach it to the loop of the bead cup and thread it on to the necklace.

This sticking method will work for anything small and round like a marble or ceramic animal head.

HOW TO MAKE A SAUSAGE DOG BROOCH

Bow wow WOW

For some people it's all about diamonds, but we prefer going to the dogs: the sausage dogs. We discovered this one (see right) in a charity shop rummage, looking well loved and a little worse for wear, but we just knew he'd look brilliant perched on a lapel of a jacket. Keep your eyes peeled the whole time. You never know when your next brooch is going to find you.

You'll need:

- A sausage dog, or any cute trinket
- A brooch back
- A glue gun
- A playing card
- A bradawl

Here's a little lost kitten from a charity shop, but now it's at home with us.

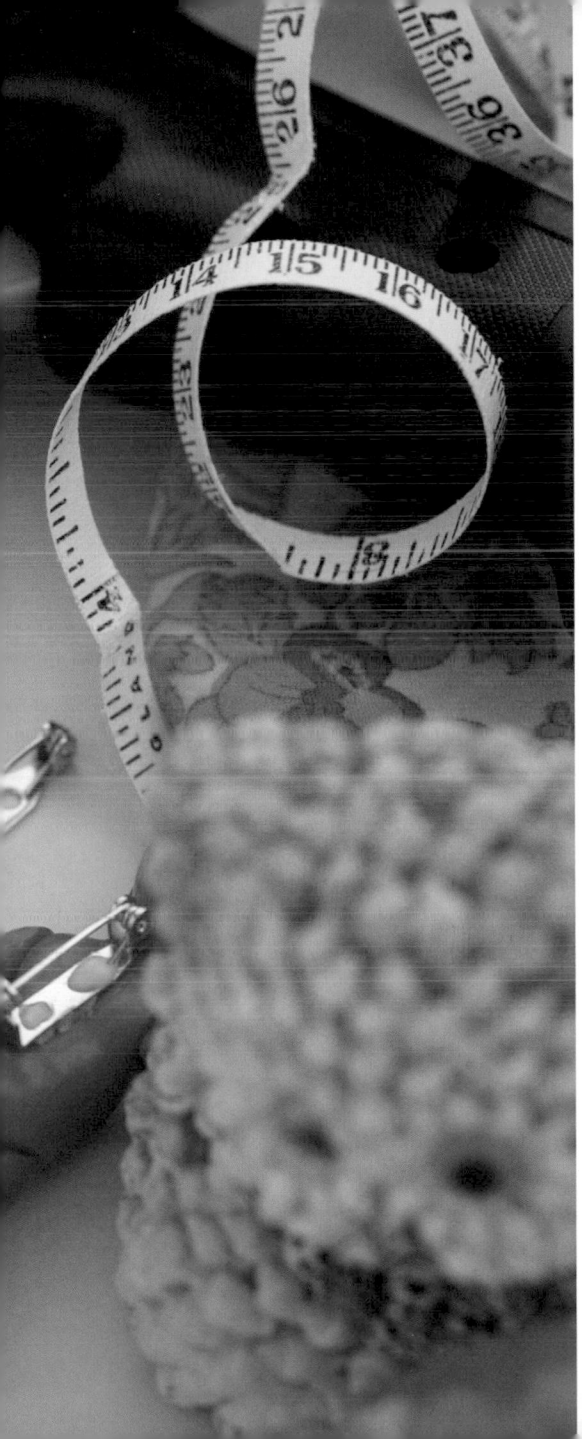

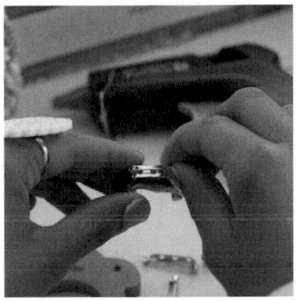

Glue guns are great – junk can be jewellery in minutes. They're also ideal for sticking a flat thing to an un-flat thing. Glue's jelly-like consistency is perfect for squidging into nooks and crannies. Surfaces should still be washed and keyed (see page 53) as glue-gun glue can be a bit rubbery when it cools and it's prone to peeling off shiny surfaces. It's also not particularly neat, so save it for places that won't be on show.

Assemble everything that you need from the get go. Then decide where you're going to glue the brooch back to the back of the sausage dog. There'll be no time for last-minute decisions!

Key the area you're going to be gluing with the bradawl.

Get the glue gun going.

When it's good and hot, squeeze the first little bit of glue on to the old flyer or playing card, so that the next squirt of glue will be just right.

Now SPEED IT UP. As soon as the glue has left the gun it will start to cool down rapidly – so get it on to the brooch back as fast as you can. Press the hot gluey brooch back on to the dog's side, and hold it there. The glue is HOT, so the pin of the brooch back is where your fingers should be. The glue will dry within seconds, ta-da! Super easy and super fast.

Clean off any unsightly blobs with white spirit, a cotton bud and elbow grease.

RIO DE JANEIRO

HOW TO MAKE A 'SOVEREIGN' RING

Worth its weight in gold

This ring is made from the smallest weight from an old set of weights and scales. They belonged to Harriet's nan, and the two of them spent many a happy hour weighing flour and mixing ingredients up. Here you're going to be mixing up glue.

You'll need:

1 brass weight - if your kitchen is lacking scales you can use a coin, a cog or a watch face

Brasso or cola (optional)

White spirit

1 disc ring shank

Bradawl

Araldite (see page 54)

Old flyer or playing card

Cocktail stick

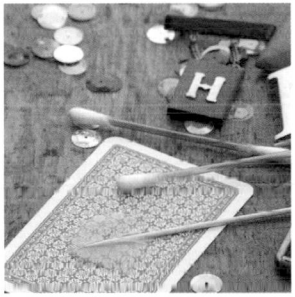

If you want a blinging look to the sovereign ring, clean the metal weight with a spot of Brasso. If you don't have any Brasso to hand, leave the weight in cola overnight, which will, amazingly, also do the job. But old and tarnished looks just fine too.

Make sure the back of the weight is super clean - white spirit will do the trick. Clean the ring shank too, and then key both with the bradawl (see page 53).

Mix up the Araldite on a flyer or playing card, using a cocktail stick. Slather a generous amount on to the back of the weight and stick it to the ring shank.

Leave to dry overnight.

HOW TO MAKE GLITTER BROOCHES

Party like the glitterati

Before we transformed the Brick Lane shop floor into a keyboard, it used to be painted with glitter. It got everywhere, on our shoes and all over our clothes. And there was even more glitter in the air when we cut up the sparkly fabric to make these badges; we really felt like we were sprinkled in stardust.

Below are four templates you can trace to make hearts, or a star-shaped brooch. To make larger ones, you need to blow them up on a photocopier or scanner.

You'll need:

- Old newspaper
- Tracing paper
- Pencil
- Card
- Scissors
- Glittery fabric
- Suede/suedette or thick felt
- Contact adhesive
- Rubber mallet (optional)
- 1 brooch back

Top TATTY Tip

If the shapes are symmetrical it doesn't matter which way you draw round your stencils on the fabric, but if you're working with letters or other non-symmetrical shapes you'll have to take a little bit more care. Mark the templates with 'F' for front and 'B' for back. On the glitter fabric the B-side should be uppermost, and on the suede the F-side. And then everything will be perfectly aligned when you come to gluing.

Contact adhesive is really flexible and works brilliantly on leather or heavy fabric. It's also madly sticky.

Open the window. Spread out old newspapers. Read the glue instructions.

Trace the templates opposite, and then transfer the design on to the card. Cut out the card hearts and stars.

On the reverse of the glittery fabric draw around the hearts and stars. Do the same on the back of the suede or the heavy felt. Cut out the shapes from the fabric.

Spread the contact adhesive glue thinly and evenly over the wrong sides of both pieces of fabric.

Leave the gluey fabric pieces and wait for a bit, according to the glue instructions.

Deep breath, steady hand. Carefully lay the glitter heart on to the suede heart, wrong sides together. Once the two gluey surfaces meet there's little chance of getting them apart again.

A gift from artist Nervous Stephen. It graced his lampshade, but now it brightens up our studio.

Press them together really hard. If you happen to have a rubber mallet handy, you could give them a whack. Trim around the edges of the heart for a clean, crisp look.

Cut a strip of suede or felt. It needs to be about 3 cm high and the inner width of your brooch back.

Place the suede or felt rectangle on to the reverse of the newly made heart and draw around it. Then spread the glue inside the rectangular shape on the heart, and on the reverse of the suede rectangle itself.

Leave for a bit, according to the glue instructions.

Undo the clasp of the brooch back, and place it back on to the gluey rectangle on the back of the heart. Then stick the suede rectangle over the brooch back, leaving the pin free.

Press down firmly, leave to dry. And get set to sparkle.

HOW TO MAKE SOME BLINGING CLIP-ON SHADES

Making the ordinary extraordinary

We couldn't believe our eyes when our friend John covered his shades in plastic crystals. We were so impressed with his bobby dazzler look that we were inspired to make our own. And it's not just glasses that look ace bedecked with crystals, you can stick them on anything – shoes, skirts, pencil cases, bags, dolls' heads, cassette tape boxes...

You'll need:

- Clip-on shades
- Assorted flatback crystals
- Beeswax
- Cocktail sticks
- Araldite (see page 54)
- Old flyer or playing card
- Soft cloth
- White spirit

Optional extras:

- Masking tape
- Felt-tip pen
- Torch or light

A teeny present from The Duke of Uke, the best ukulele shop in town.

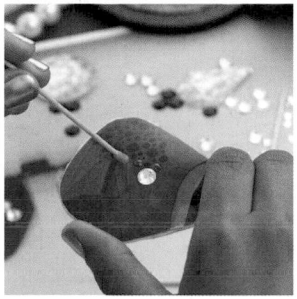

Clean the glasses in warm soapy water.

Pile the different shades and sizes of crystals in front of you and ponder some patterns: think diagonals, concentric circles or swirls, and then imagine them stuck to your shades. You could scan the clip-on shades, print out a life-size image and practise laying out your design; but remember your flat pattern will look different on a curved surface. Take a photo to remind you of what you're planning to do.

Before you start gluing you could stick masking tape to the reverse of the shades and felt tip your pattern onto the masking tape so you have a guide-line to follow. You might have to shine a light through the lenses to see the felt tip clearly.

Or just throw caution to the wind and get going.

Mix up a small batch of Araldite and armed with a cut-off cocktail stick dot the glue on where you want each crystal to gleam. Do a few spots at a time.

Stick a blob of beeswax to the end of another cut-off cocktail stick. This is a really easy way of picking up the crystals and popping them on the glue.

Pick up the crystals with the cut-off cocktail stick loaded with beeswax. Keep dotting and sticking until your pattern is complete. If you're gluing crystals to a curved surface, you'll need to work in stages so that the bit you're gluing is level. Rotate, reposition, leave to dry. And repeat. It sounds more tricky to say than to do

And then repeat all the steps on the reverse of the shades. Try and keep the crystals perfectly aligned on the back and the front, or you'll have a slim chance of being able to see through them.

Leave to dry, and then polish with a soft cloth and a dash of white spirit.

B B B BLING.

HOW TO MAKE JIGSAW PUZZLE EARRINGS

A little piece of my heart

We spent a lot of time on holiday and at art college doing jigsaw puzzles, just staring at the colours and shapes, before getting around to finishing them. Every charity shop has a pile of vintage jigsaws, often with pieces missing, which are perfect for transforming into jewellery. Earrings are simple. Make a pair to match every outfit in your wardrobe.

We love jigsaws, and we love France.

Top TATTY Tip

Some old and beautiful wooden jigsaws have hidden shapes in the puzzle, like the ones in this picture. If you are lucky enough to discover one, keep it safe, as they can be turned into perfect pendants and brooches.

You'll need:

- 2 pieces from an old jigsaw, wood if you're lucky, but cardboard will do (cardboard earrings will be a bit more flimsy, and not rainproof!)
- Old newspaper
- Gloss varnish
- Paintbrush
- Wet and dry sandpaper
- Cloth or a piece of old fabric
- Pencil
- Silver earring posts
- Araldite (see page (54)
- Old flyer or playing card
- Cocktail stick

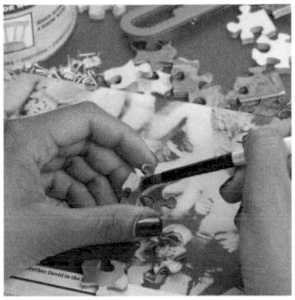

Before you get started have a TATTY style ponder of your puzzle. Think about the colours and shapes, and how they'll work as pairs. Look out for interesting bits – faces, flowers or little animals look immediately cute, but you might have to play around with other pieces to come up with a look you like.

When you've decided, lay your pieces out on a newspaper, and give the front of the pieces a light coat of varnish using the paintbrush. Leave them to dry in a nice, clean place: you don't want dust bedevilling all your hard work!

When they've dried, add another coat of varnish, and let that dry too. Then varnish the sides too.

Have a quick over-view of the dried pieces, and get to work with the wet and dry sandpaper if you spot any flecks, flaws or specks in the freshly varnished surface. Hold the jigsaw puzzle piece with your fingers and put the wet and dry sandpaper on a flat surface and gently rub the puzzle pieces against the sandpaper.

Wipe away the varnish dust with a cloth. The jigsaw pieces should be nice and shiny after two coats, but if you want them to be really glossy, recoat, and repeat the steps above.

Turn the pieces over. Pencil mark where you're going to glue the earring post. For the earrings to sit nicely the earring post needs to be glued in the top half of the jigsaw piece.

Mix up the Araldite with a cocktail stick – make sure you give it a good old stir. Apply the glue to the earring posts, and then stick the earring posts to the puzzle pieces, using the pencil marks as a guide. Leave them on a flat surface to dry overnight. If the surface isn't flat, you may find the earring posts have slid right off, and that's not the look you were looking for.

Hole-y moley

We have made necklaces from wooden mobile phone bottle openers and a massive macramé owl wall hanging.

Sometimes the hole is already there, like our Eiffel Tower charm belts. They were made from touristy key rings that we'd discovered in Paris. Rosie used to head off on the Eurostar and haggle in bad French for the best deals, and then we'd whip off the key ring bit and let them dangle from the leather. To test if your ornament will look good as a necklace thread it on to some ribbon. Some things will flop, hang in an odd way, or flip over. Or they could go sideways, or just be generally lop sided. A jump ring can solve many a problem. Attach a jump ring to the hole in the ornament, and then thread the jump ring to the necklace.

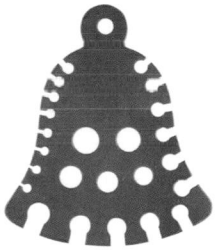

A knitting gauge is always handy, especially when it's this super cute.

A lovely keepsake from a special cake.

A find from a Parisian flea market. Oo la la.

HOW TO MAKE A TAPE MEASURE ROSETTE

Inch by inch...

We've always loved tape measures. In our sewing kits are old vintage tape measures, in shades of baby blue and pale yellow, which once belonged to our grannies and our mums. Every time we see one in a charity shop we have to buy it to add to our collections, even if we know we're never going to use them to actually measure anything. They're perfect for making a fluttering curtain for a doorway, but with a bit of folding and pinning they can also be transformed into pretty star-shaped rosettes, which will get people talking. Rosie was even given a free steak by the local butcher when she wore her rosette into his shop, so impressed was he with her dapper brooch.

You'll need:

- 1 tape measure
- 2 split pin paper fasteners
- Hand-held hole punch (if you don't have a hole punch you can use the prong of the kilt pin to poke the holes)
- Pair of sharp scissors
- 1 kilt pin or safety pin
- 1 pair of flat nose pliers

Optional extras:

- Small piece of felt
- Blob of contact adhesive
- Embroidery thread and a needle

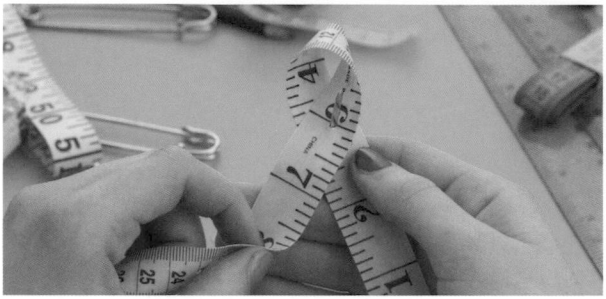

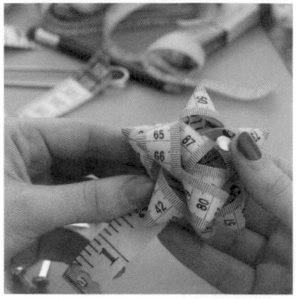

Smooth the tape measure out, and go to work on the inches side. You'll be using both metric and imperial measurements in this make, so pay attention!

Start by punching 2 mm size holes at 3-inch intervals along the middle of the tape measure, starting at number 3, and stopping at number 33. Now make three more holes at numbers 35, 37 and 39. As you're working, give the hole punch a little twist as you squeeze down, so that the little circle of plastic will pop out the back as you press.

Grab hold of one of the split pin paper fasteners, and poke it through the tape measure at number 3. The pinhead goes on the centimetres side.

Now for some loops. Give the tape measure a little twist and then pop the newly made loop on to the paper fastener at hole number 6. Oh, and make sure that the inches side of the tape measure is ALWAYS facing upwards; this is the side where the paper fastener prongs are sticking out.

Keep twisting and popping the loops on to the paper fastener at every hole, at those 3-inch intervals, and always heading and twisting in the same direction.

When you've made five loops, do a little preening, and even them out into a nice star shape.

If it is not a nice star shape you have probably not twisted the same way every time. Undo and start over.

And off you go again. Make another five loops in the same way. The points of this star should fall between the points of your first star. A bit more preening wouldn't go amiss.

Hurray, you've arrived at number 33 on the inches side of the tape measure. Now for the smaller inner loops. Make three smaller loops, and pop them, one after the other, on the pin fastener. This time you're not heading for the stars, a triangle is the shape you're after. This is going to be the centre of the rosette. Snip off the excess tape measure with a pair of sharp scissors, at 39¼ inches. Cut at a jaunty angle, because it looks pretty. Don't throw it away: you're going to need it in a sec.

Take hold of the second of the split pin fasteners, and push it through the centre of the rosette. This will make the first fastener pop out, and (ta-da!) the prongs will now be at the back.

Cut 6 inches from the excess snipped-off bit of the tape measure. Make sure you use the end with the metal bit, and fold it in half. Give it a little twist, so that the two strands sit apart, and at an angle. This is the tail of the rosette. Drape the strands over the bar of the kilt pin that doesn't open, otherwise when you come to pin it to the neck of your snazzy jumper you won't be able to!

Grab the hole punch again, and punch a hole through both strands of the tail, close to the kilt pin. Then pop the folded tail, with the kilt pin, on to the reverse of your rosette.

Squash the prongs of the split pin fastener down firmly with the pliers, so that everything is held securely in place. You're mostly done, but for a prettier finish you could:

Glue a piece of felt over the back of the pin fastener, with contact adhesive. This will stop it snagging your jumper. If you're feeling really fancy, sew your name on to the felt before you glue; it'll look just like a lovely label. Or you could even embroider a message on to the felt if you're giving the rosette as a gift.

Some tape measures have ditched their imperial side and gone entirely metric. If you're working with centimetres, here's where you punch the holes: start at 8 cm, then punch every 8 cm, but STOP at 88 cm, and punch three extra holes at 93, 98 and 103. Cut the tape measure at 104 cm – the tail should be about 20 cm long.

Top TATTY Tip

Your rosette could become an ornament for a necklace. Make up the rosette as above, but call a halt before you add on the tail and the kilt pin. Grab hold of a pair of round-nose pliers and, instead of pushing apart the prongs on the split pin fastener, smooth them together with the pliers. Bend the prongs down with the pliers, and then roll them up in a tight little circle. Then attach a jump ring and thread it to a necklace.

With a bit of practice you could make a rosette in ten minutes. And you don't just have to use tape measures. What about ribbon rosettes? You'll need to pencil the measurements on to the ribbon, and then get looping. Bear in mind if you're using tiny ribbons, the holes should be closer together, and further apart if you're working with a massive ribbon.

And if you want the rosette to be mega-large, use ribbon that's much longer than 39 inches and keep making loops until the rosette is as big and fat as an ornamental cabbage, but not so big that you can't close the pin fastener. Thinner ribbon will give you the best result. Try these measurements for a brilliant effect on about 2.5 metres of 20mm ribbon: 6 holes every 10 cm, 5 every 9 cm, 5 every 8 cm and 5 every 7 cm and 5 every 5 cm and 3 at 3 cm.

Top TATTY Tip

You could continue the centimetres and inches theme and make yourself a tape measure belt to match your tape measure rosette. Get an old white belt and a black permanent marker, and draw on the inches by hand. It doesn't have to be accurate; in fact the further apart your inches are, the narrower your waist will appear when you do the belt up.

This vintage tape measure was Rosie's granny's.

HOW TO MAKE A SHRINKY NECKLACE

Good things come in small (crisp) packages

We ate so many bags of cheap crisps when we made these shrinky necklaces to sell in the shop. Hundreds! And we became obsessed by the packaging, and the amazing graphics on noodle packets and sweet wrappers from continental markets. One day we found an ancient empty crisp packet – hedgehog flavour – under the floorboards and it was like discovering gold!

You'll need:

- Old food packets, not foiled or metallic
- 1 chain necklace (see page 36)
- Greaseproof paper
- Baking sheet
- Damp tea towel, in case of fire-related emergencies
- Old tea towel
- Hand-held hole punch
- 1 regular jump ring
- 2 pairs of flat-nose pliers

A Moldy Peaches ticket, the perfect band to shrink crisp bags to.

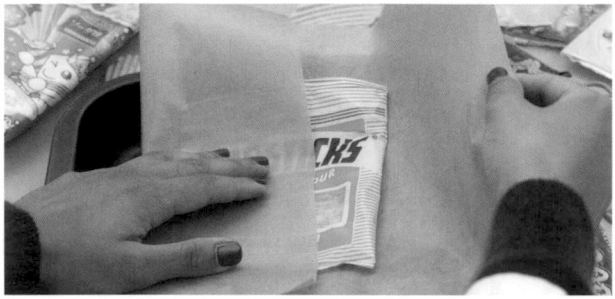

Scoff the contents of the packets while making up the necklace. Salt and vinegar crisps, yum.

Make an envelope with the greaseproof paper and pop your food packet inside it. Set your oven to a medium heat and let it warm up a bit. Put the envelopes on to a baking tray and put it in the oven. Don't wander off. The packets will start to shrink and curl up but you don't want them to burn or blister, so keep a weather eye on proceedings.

As soon as you think they've shrunk enough, remove the baking sheet and quickly pop a folded tea towel on top of the envelope and then slam your hand down on it to flatten your shrinkies. BAM! Such a satisfying noise.

Don't worry if it goes wrong the first few times you attempt it, as there's a bit of a knack to it. Practise on easy-to-come-by stuff, and when you've mastered the art, go to work on your carefully hoarded vintage packages.

Now decide how you want your shrinky to dangle. If you punch a hole in the corner it'll hang aslant, but if you punch a hole in the top centre it'll dangle straight down. Use the hole punch to make the hole when you've chosen its position.

Open a regular jump ring with the pliers and thread the packet on to the jump ring and then the jump ring to the necklace. Close with the pliers.

SMITHS
CHIPSTICKS
SALT 'N VINEGAR FLAVOUR
MAIZE & POTATO SNACK
MAIZE & POTATO SNACK
8794
ESS
BEAUTY CARE
PARTY TIME
30's Birt

Bassetts
Jelly Babies
Natural
made with real fruit juice
Maynards
gums
Galaxy
Galaxy
Galaxy
Galaxy
Galaxy
Galaxy
Galaxy
Galaxy
Galaxy
46g
.60p

KOPIKO
CAPPUCCINO
Cadbury
DAIRY MILK
Caramel
Nibbles
ROWNTREE'S
Fruit
Pastilles
£1
Bassetts

HOW TO MAKE A HORSE BRASS NECKLACE

Bold as brass

Any horse-brass-type ornament would look good for this necklace – anchors or nautical shapes are lovely, but you might be lucky enough to find one of a local cathedral or castle. But do go for one that has holes in it already, as they're really too heavy to glue.

You'll need:

- 1 pendant-length brass necklace, approx 80 cm long (see page 37)
- 1 large jump ring
- 2 pairs of flat-nose pliers
- 1 brass palette or similar horse-brass

Make up the necklace.

Open the large jump ring with the pliers.

Thread the chain and the brass palette through the jump ring, and then close the jump ring with the pliers.

Look what happens when you don't use a jump ring (see left).

An old horse brass from the Isle of Wight, where Rosie grew up.

HOW TO MAKE A MUSICAL NOTE CHARM BRACELET

Take note

When we first started Tatty Devine we'd pile into Rosie's old Mini and scour cake shops across the land, looking for cool decorations. We found some great little decorations in a shop on a housing estate precinct in Portsmouth, which we made into charm bracelets and earrings, but we also love these musical notes, which we bought from one of our favourite shops, Party, Party in Dalston – so good they named it twice.

For a simple make choose shapes wih holes in already like these.

You'll need:

18 cm trace chain bracelet (see page 36)

Several treble clef or a semi-quaver cake decorations

2 pairs of flat-nose pliers

Regular jump rings, one for each 'charm'

Make up the bracelet.

Try it on. Just right? Hurray. Too tight, add a leader. Too loose, get the wire cutters out.

Count the links on the chain so you can space out your cake charms nice and evenly. For example, if your bracelet has 25 links, then put the notes on links 3, 7, 11, 15, 19 and 23.

Grab hold of the pliers and the jump rings and attach the charms along the length of the bracelet.

You can add as many as you like, or keep adding to it as you find more fab stuff with holes in.

Top TATTY Tip

If you want your notes to be black then get the spray paint out. Open the window, or head outside. Get rid of dirt or grease with warm, soapy water, and let the notes dry out. When they're dry, spray the front with undercoat, which helps paint stick to plastic. Let it dry and then spray the back. Let that dry too. Then get going with the black spray paint. Cover the front, let it dry and then spray the back and let that dry too. Make up a jaunty tune to accompany your back-to-black musical notes.

PAI

Drill bits and pieces

A cast-off piece of wood discovered in Pam's place in Bridport.

Don't fear the drill. You need to take care, but once you get going you can put a hole in almost anything, just not your fingers!

♣ Safety goggles are always a good idea, as is tying your hair back. Long hair twisted around a drill is no fun. Ditch scarves, ties and any dangly necklaces and bracelets too, before you start drilling

♦ Cover your mouth with a mask: plastic or wood dust is not nice to breathe in.

♥ If you're worried about scratching the surface of your lovely trinket, smooth on a bit of masking tape, and pencil mark where you want to drill. Then whip it off when you're done.

♠ Hold the items that you're drilling firmly so they don't spin out of control, and always drill straight down. Take your time.

♥ Things can get hot, so if possible use a clamp or a vice, as that way your fingers won't get burned. Ouch.

♣ Invest in some beeswax. It's a great lubricant: dab the drill bit with it and it'll make everything smoother.

A Rough and Ready Guide to Drill Bit Sizes

Your drill bit size is related to the size of the jump rings you're using, and the thickness of the thing you're going to drill. If you're drilling through thin things, like plectrums, go for a drill bit that's slightly bigger than the wire the jump ring is made of. So with a 5 mm jump ring that's made of 1.6 mm wire, go for a 1.8 mm drill bit. Or if you're drilling through something that's thicker than 4 mm, use a bigger jump ring and a 3 mm drill bit. But the best way to work out your jump-ring-to-drill relationship is to test it out. Drill on a scrappy bit of something that's the same thickness as your chosen object. The jump ring should move freely in the drilled hole, so adjust the size of the jump ring and the drill bit until you find a good fit. Oh, and if you're drilling into something flat, think about where the hole should go before you drill. Too close to the edge, and it'll snap; too far away, and the jump ring won't reach. With the simple addition of a hole, a junk shop find can be transformed into a cool Friday night accessory. There's a whole world of ornaments out there that would be better as jewellery, rather than gathering dust on the mantelpiece. As Rosie often says: 'Make a shelf of yourself.'

Puzzles are great for long journeys, especially if your phone's run out of batteries.

HOW TO MAKE A PLECTRUM BRACELET AND NECKLACE

I should be so plucky, plucky, plucky...

Plectrums were one of the first 'found' objects that we turned into jewellery. It was quite a revelation! Harriet shared a Brick Lane flat with a band, and the boys left guitar plectrums everywhere.

When we had cleared out their stash we headed down to Denmark Street and braved the cute rock boys who worked behind the music shop counter. It was great listening to them recount stories about the gigs they'd been to the night before and how hungover they were, while we picked out what colour plectrums we wanted.

It made us want to be in a band too. We even had a few rehearsals in the Brick Lane studio, though we never played a gig. But every time Rosie went to see a band she used to steal their plectrums from the stage and add them to her charm bracelet.

If you can't nick them from a band, you can buy all sorts online at www.guitarplectrums.co.uk. Plectrums come in loads of bright colours, but there are also tortoise shell ones, clear ones, wooden ones and ones printed with pictures – an endless array of loveliness.

Here are the instructions for a charm bracelet and necklace, but once you've got these skills under your belt, the world's your oyster. Go crazy and put plectrums on anything you can think of: earrings, belts, key rings, light pulls...

There are hundreds of different colour plectrums in the Denmark Street music shops.

A much-prized plectrum stolen from our house mates, the band Duke Spirit.

You'll need:

Assorted guitar plectrums

Pen or pencil

Leftover bit of wood,
or something you don't mind drilling holes in

Drill

1.8 mm drill bit

2 pairs of flat-nose pliers

Regular jump rings,
one for each plectrum

For the bracelet:

A thick trace chain bracelet
(see page 36)

For the necklace:

A 40cm necklace
(see page 36)

Make up the bracelet.

Have a play around with the plectrums to see which colours work best together. Once you have got your colourway going on, think about how you want the plectrums to hang. They'll dangle differently depending on where you drill. We've chosen to drill in the middle.

Drill one plectrum at a time. Pen or pencil a dot where you want the hole to go. Place the scrappy bit of wood on a sturdy surface, and then firmly hold the plectrum down with your pointing finger. Drill a hole, and pick off any little bits of plastic that might have been left behind. You want nice, clean circles.

Oh, and if you drill the top and the bottom of the plectrum, you'll be able to link more than one plectrum together.

If you don't have a drill, you could have a go with a hole punch. It's trickier, though, as plectrums have a tendency to crack under hole-punch pressure. Best solution? Find a DIY friend and borrow their drill. You can make them a plectrum accessory as a thank-you present.

Now for a little spacey interlude. Count the links on your chain. For the plectrums to hang nicely, it's important to hang them on the same side of the link all the way along the bracelet. So, for example, if your chain is 25 links long, start in 3 links from the end, and put jump rings on every other link, so you can attach 11 evenly spaced plectrums. If you want your bracelet to be less jangly, then put jump rings on links 3, 7, 11, 15, 19 and 23, and attach 6 plectrums. Or you could go for a mega plectrum bracelet with one on every link, but make sure that all the links are always on the same side of the chain.

OK? Lay out the plectrums in the order you want them attached to the bracelet. Grab both pairs of pliers and the regular jump rings and attach the plectrums to the chain.

Make up the necklace.

Mark up the plectrums and drill holes in them, as described above. Attach a regular jump ring to each plectrum and close it up tightly with the pliers.

Thread the plectrums on to the chain. Make sure the plectrums are facing out the right way.

Top TATTY Tip

Plectrum jewellery is always cool, and handy too! If you're the guitarist in a band and you're missing a plectrum, you can always unthread one and strum on.

Tatty
Devine
Tatty
Devine

HOW TO MAKE A KEYBOARD NECKLACE

I'm with the band

We love, love, love keyboards. We've made keyboard belts and ties, and the floor of the Brick Lane shop has a keyboard painted on it. It makes us think of the Blondie LP *Parallel Lines*, with Debbie Harry in a white dress, the boys in the band dressed in black and a black-and-white-striped background. Have your own musical moment with this pitch-perfect keyboard necklace.

You'll need:

60 cm necklace (see page 36)	Masking tape
1 small toy piano	Pencil
Small screwdriver	Drill
Hacksaw	1.8 mm drill bit
File	Scrappy bit of wood
Wet and dry sandpaper	2 pairs of flat-nose pliers
	Regular jump rings, one for each piano key

Make up your necklace.

Take the toy piano apart and remove the white and black keys with the small screwdriver.

If the keyboard keys are moulded together, separate them by sawing through the plastic with the hacksaw.

File off any sharpness and then smooth the edges with the wet and dry sandpaper. Put the sandpaper face up on a flat surface, and gently rub the piano keys against it.

Turn the keyboard the wrong side up, cover it with masking tape and mark where you want to drill with the pencil.

Fit the drill with a 1.8 mm drill bit and then carefully drill through each key. Remember to put a scrappy bit of wood under the keys so that you don't accidentally drill through the kitchen table. When you've finished drilling, remove the masking tape.

Lay the piano keys out the way you want them to hang on the necklace.

Holding the necklace at the clasp, work out where the centre of your necklace is. Pop the middle piano key on to the centre of the necklace with a regular jump ring and the pliers.

Working from the centre out in each direction add a jump-ringed piano key on every other link, on the same side of the chain, until all the charms are used up.

This mini keyboard reminds us of Snoopy cartoons, with a soundtrack by Schroeder.

HOW TO MAKE A THREEPENNY BIT NECKLACE

Find a penny and pick it up

We love a bit of rhyming slang so when we found this threepenny bit ('thrupp'ny bits' are, um, tits) we had to make it into a necklace. But any old coin would work – old ten-pence pieces look massive compared to modern ones, and an old franc necklace would be perfect attire for listening to Serge Gainsbourg, or watching *À Bout de Souffle* on the sofa.

Who doesn't love free stuff, especially when it's given to us by friends.

You'll need:

- 60 cm fine chain necklace (see page 36)
- 1 threepenny bit (or another old money coin)
- Masking tape
- Pencil
- Scrappy bit of wood
- Clamp
- Bradawl
- Hammer
- Drill
- High-speed steel 2 mm drill bit
- Beeswax block
- 1 jump ring
- 2 pairs of flat-nose pliers

Peruse your glorious threepenny bit and decide where you're going to drill. Head or crest to the front? Focus on the lettering? These are the things you need to consider before making a hole.

You'll need to drill at least 2 to 3 mm in from the edge of the coin. The hole is going to be 2 mm in diameter, so you need a bit of leeway. It's a good idea to stick a little bit of masking tape to the coin and mark it with a pencil, as a guide. Handily the masking tape will also help to protect your coin if your drilling hand slips when you get going.

Align the tip of the bradawl with your pencil mark and bash the bradawl with the hammer. This little hole will act as a guide for the drill bit.

Pop the scrappy bit of wood underneath the coin, and clamp them together to a sturdy surface or a workbench. The coin gets really hot when you're drilling, so the clamp will save you from burned fingers.

Start the drill, and dip the tip of the drill bit in the beeswax block. You'll need to do this at regular intervals. Start to drill the hole in the coin, slowly and gently. If you're doing it right, you should see little flecks of coin spreading over the workbench; if not, then push a little bit harder, but always remember the beeswax, and keep the pace slow. Too much friction and heat will temper the coin and make it harder to drill.

When you reach the far side of the coin, pull the drill out while it's still rotating so that it doesn't get stuck.

Unclamp the coin, and hey! A hole. Careful, it might be hot.

Attach it to the necklace with the jump ring and the pliers.

But don't stop there: get drilling and add more treasure trove coins to the necklace. Or you could drill holes in each end of the coins and link them together with jump rings to make coin chain bracelets or necklaces or belts.

Top TATTY Tip

If you want to make a coin necklace, but are put off by all the drilling, head to the DIY shop and pick up one of these.

Clean and key the back of the coin (see page 53) and the back of the D-loop. Mix up some Araldite (see page 54), stick them together and leave them to dry overnight. Use the handy little wire to thread it to your necklace.

HOW TO MAKE A WOODEN MUSHROOM NECKLACE

Touch wood

We are nuts about anything that's wood effect. Show us a wood-look belt, fabric or sticky-back plastic and we're there. But we LOVE real wood too. Owls, squirrels, birds, toadstools – basically anything that you find in a woodland that's been carved out of wood – make our hearts skip a beat. Especially when they're transformed into necklaces. You can paint them. Or keep them *au naturel* with polish and varnish.

Harriet's giant clothes peg, bought from a garage sale in Joshua Tree, USA.

You'll need:

- A small wooden object, like our lovely mushroom
- Wet and dry sandpaper
- Danish oil
- Paintbrush
- Soft cloth
- Pencil
- Drill
- 0.8 mm drill bit
- Blob of Araldite (see page 54)
- Old flyer or playing card
- Cocktail stick
- 1 screw-in eyelet
- 1 pair of flat-nose pliers
- Shoelaces or ribbon

Wash away the wood's grubbiness with some warm soapy water.

If it looks a little lacklustre, rub it down with wet and dry sandpaper, and add a little Danish oil to the grain. Danish oil gives a lovely, light satin sheen to wood, and it's subtler than varnish because it seeps into the wood, rather than just coating it. Paint it on to the wood, use a soft cloth to remove the excess oil, and then rub some more so it gently glows.

Pencil mark where you're going to drill on top of the mushroom.

Drill a pilot hole, about 3–4 mm deep, straight down. Dust off any sawdust. This hole is a guide for the screw-in eyelet, so the pilot hole should be smaller than the screw, and with luck it will prevent the wood from cracking as you're not forcing the metal through the grain.

Mix up the Araldite on a spare flyer or playing card using the cocktail stick. Put a blob of glue on the end of the eyelet, pop the eyelet into the drilled hole and twist it. Keep turning the eyelet until it's snugly fitted into the wood. Use pliers to hold the eyelet if it feels tricky.

Thread the shoelace through the eyelet and fasten it with a knot. Make sure it is long enough to go over your head so you don't have to undo it.

A pack of vintage buttons, that remind us of dice. We love how they look.

HOW TO MAKE A TINY FRUIT MACHINE DICE NECKLACE

Tutti frutti

We've whiled away many a rainy hour with board games, jigsaw puzzles and Boggle tournaments. And any time we saw a travel chess set, we bought it; the tiny pieces made perfect dangly earrings or charms. The same holds true for stray pieces, like this neat little fruit dice, from those wet-weather board games. Find a random assortment of bits and bobs and get drilling.

You'll need:

1 fine-chain necklace (see page 36)	Araldite (see page 54)
1 small, cute object: we've used a vintage dice	Old flyer or playing card
Drill	Cocktail stick
0.8 mm drill bit	Bowl of uncooked rice
Blu-Tack	1 regular jump ring
Wire cutters	2 pairs of flat-nose pliers
1 eye pin	

Small and cute objects need small and cute findings. An eye pin – the more delicate cousin of the screw-in eyelet – is the way to go.

Make up the necklace.

Decide which corner of the dice you want to drill, depending on how you want it to hang.

Hold the dice and drill down about 4 mm. If it feels wobbly, put a blob of Blu-Tack on a flat surface and put the dice on top of that to keep it steady.

Using the wire cutters snip the eye pin so there's around 4 mm of wire left.

Top TATTY Tip

You could set eye pins in the opposite corners of lots of dice, and string them together to make a pretty bracelet.

Pop the eye pin into the drilled hole to try it for size. The loop on the pin should be flush with the dice. If it isn't, do a bit more snipping with the wire cutter.

Mix up the Araldite on a flyer or playing card, using the cocktail stick. Dip the eye pin end into the glue and then pop it back into the drilled hole.

Make sure you set the eye pin in so that your pendant will hang to the front and not twist around.

Leave to dry overnight, standing upright in a bowl of rice.

When it's dry, open a small jump ring with the pliers and attach it to the eye of the eye pin, and then thread it on to the necklace.

77

Making a spectacle of yourself

We love glasses...

Rosie used to make works of art with them but she only used the lenses, so there were loads of frames scattered around the studio. It made us wonder what else you could do with them. Years later they inspired our acrylic glasses necklaces, but why not make your own DIY version, and look super-smart? There's nothing like a bit of secretary chic.

Eye eye, just waiting for a dab of glue and a brooch back.

HOW TO MAKE GLASSES NECKLACES

Fix up, look sharp

Try hunting for old glasses in car boot sales or charity shops. We especially favour frames from old-style glasses, vintage shades, NHS spectacles, and the sort of glasses that Jarvis Cocker or your granny would wear.

A saucy dart flight from a trophy shop in Whitstable, bought on a very rainy day.

You'll need:

- 1 pair of old glasses
- Soft cloth
- Cotton buds
- Bench vice
- Hacksaw
- Small flat file
- Drill
- 1.2 mm drill bit
- Araldite (see page 54)
- Old flyer or playing card
- Cocktail sticks
- 2 small screw-in eyelets
- 60 cm necklace (see page 36)
- Wire cutters
- Regular jump rings
- 2 pairs of flat-nose pliers

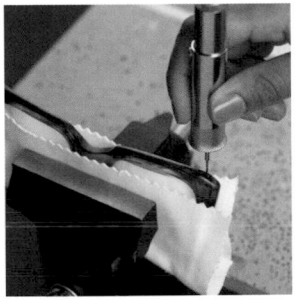

Old spectacles frames are often really dirty when you first come across them, like all the best treasure. But don't be put off: a good clean will get rid of years of accumulated grime. Warm, soapy water is the best. Harsh cleaners can corrode some old types of plastic and may strip away any lovely details that are painted or printed on the frames.

Use a soft cloth to avoid scratches and get busy with cocktail sticks and cotton buds to get into all the nooks and crannies.

When the clean-up is done and dusted, remove the arms of the glasses. Hold the glasses securely in a vice and, using the hacksaw, cut through the hinges as close to the frame as possible.

Using the file, smooth off any sharp edges. These will be against your skin so the smoother the better.

Hold the frames in the vice, and drill a hole approximately 3 mm deep into the top corner of the glasses frame, using the 1.2 mm size drill bit. Make sure you don't hit the lenses or the metal inside the frames. Do the same on the other side.

Mix up the Araldite on a flyer or playing card, using the cocktail stick. Dab a small blob of glue on to the screw-in eyelets and then screw them into the holes on the frame. Leave to dry.

Make up the necklace; it looks best if it is long enough for you to hold the chain up to your face. Hold up the necklace by the clasp and, using the wire cutters, cut it in half, opposite the clasp.

Attach the chain to the regular jump rings with the pliers, and then the jump rings to the eyelets. Pop it over your head, and *voilà* – simple library chic.

Plain and simple is lovely, but if you want something a bit more snazzy, there's a world of possibilities. Cartoon eyes look great.

You need masking tape, Araldite and its accoutrements, and some little, tiny, flat-back black crystals. (Not only will they look amazing, they also make a genius tongue twister, tiny, flat-back black crystals, tiny, flat-back black crystals...)

Have a quick peruse of a cartoon for some inspiration. Stick masking tape pupil shapes to the back of each lens, cartoon-style. On the front of the shades, carefully glue the black crystals, following the masking tape shape (see page 53 for gluing instructions).

You'll go a bit googly-eyed with all the sticking, but it'll be so worth it. Leave to dry overnight. Peel off the masking tape, clean any stray blobs of glue with white spirit and cotton buds, and eye eye, you're ready for your starry close-up.

HOW TO MAKE A PEARL GLASSES NECKLACE

The world is your oyster

You'll need:

1 pair of old glasses (children's work well)	Araldite (see page 54)	Superglue
	Old flyer or playing card	Needlework scissors
Soft cloth	Cocktail stick	4 calottes
Cotton buds	2 small screw-in eyelets or cut-off head pins	81 4 mm pearls or beads
Bench vice		4 eye pins
Hacksaw	1 packet of no. 10/0.9 mm natural silk beading thread (buy the sort that has the needle already attached)	Wire cutters
Small flat file		1 pair of round-nose pliers
Drill		1 head pin
0.8 mm drill bit	4 crimps	6 small jump rings
	2 pairs of flat-nose pliers	1 lobster clasp

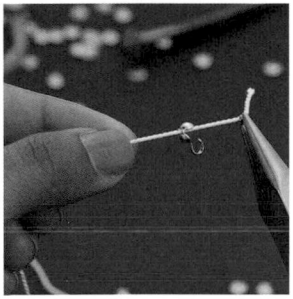

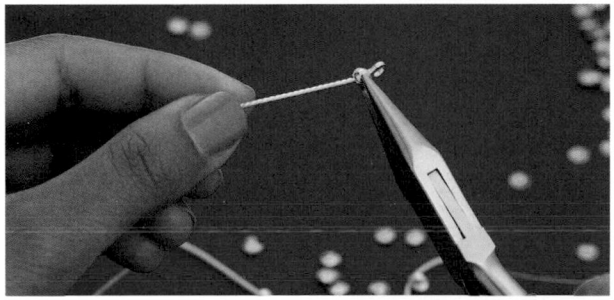

If you can find an old pair of children's glasses for this necklace, they will give you a pretty, petite look. If not, adult specs will still look spectacular.

Follow the instructions up to attaching the chain in the How to Make Glasses Necklaces make (p 107).

Take the beading silk and tie a knot 10 mm from the end. Thread on a crimp right up to the knot.

Squash the crimp with the flat-nose pliers as above. Dab a tiny blob of superglue on to the knot. Let it dry, then snip off the thread end, as close to the knot as you can, with the needlework scissors.

Thread on a calotte, and squish it round the crimp.

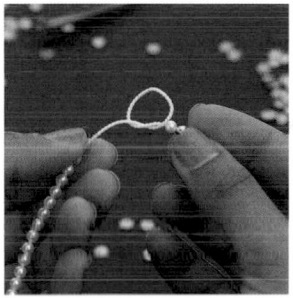

Things are about to get knotty. Thread on 38 pearls, leaving about 10 cm before the calotte, so that you've got room to tie a knot on the string without the pearls getting in the way.

Slide one pearl down to the calotte, and tie a knot in the silk, right up tight to the bead so it's nice and secure. Use the end of the silk with the calotte on for working the knot.

Slide the next pearl down to the freshly tied knot, and tie another knot as close as you can get, after the new pearl. Make sure the knots are really tight, and the pearls are as close as possible. Keep on sliding and knotting until there's only one pearl left. This time it's not a knot you're after, but a calotte.

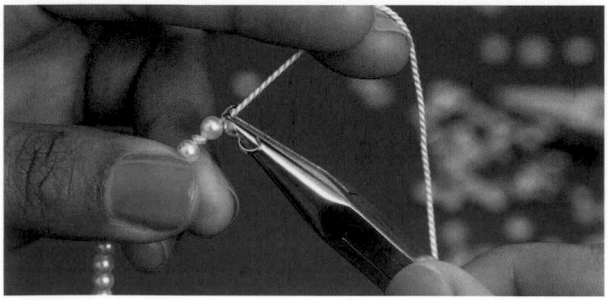

Thread the calotte on, followed by a crimp. Hold the crimp firmly with the tip of the pliers, but don't squash it. Next pull on the silk beading thread, and push down with the pliers so that the calotte and the crimp are not even a hair's breath away from the last pearl. Happy? Then squash that crimp!

Tie a knot right next to the crimp, dab a spot of superglue on to the knot, wait until it's dry and then trim the thread with the needlework scissors. Then squish the calotte around them so it's all nicely sealed in place.

Make yourself another strand of pearls to match the first one.

Gently pull on the strands of pearls to unkink any kinks. Now for a fancy fastening. Grab hold of the remaining five pearls, plus four eye pins and one head pin. Pop one pearl on to one eye pin. Trim the wire, with the wire cutters, so that there's about 10 mm sticking out. Then bend the wire down at a right angle with the flat-nose pliers. With the round-nose pliers roll the wire up into a loop, with tiny twists, rolling away from you. Try to get it to roughly the same size as the loop at the other end.

As a rough rule, the closer the wire is to the handle of the round-nose pliers, the bigger the loops are going to be, so for a large loop grip the wire towards the handles, and for a smaller loop grip the wire towards the tip.

Then holding each loop with the flat-nose pliers, check that both loops are facing in the same direction. Tweak gently if they aren't. Repeat with three more pearls.

Top TATTY Tip

You could make this pearly necklace for your real glasses. Make one very long strand of pearls using this technique, and add regular jump rings to each end. Head along to the opticians and buy two rubber spectacle holders, and attach your strand of glam pearls to them.

Pop the fifth pearl on to the head pin, trim and roll the wire in exactly the same way.

Link all these pearls together with five small jump rings to make a little string of pearls. And then join the jump ring end of the little string of pearls to one of the main strands of pearls. If your calotte is lacking a loop, roll up its wire in the exact same way as the head pin.

On the other strand, attach the lobster clasp with the last small jump ring. The clasp should comfortably fit anywhere on to the little string of pearls, which means your necklace is adjustable. Hurray.

Then attach a pearl strand to each side of the glasses frame, to the screw-in eyelets, making sure that the clasp is in your right hand when you put the necklace on (assuming you're right-handed). Aah. Pretty as a picture.

Make an accessory of an accessory. These tiny specs belonged to a toy doll.

HOW TO MAKE A SNAZZY SUNGLASSES NECKLACE

Shady lady

Modern sunglasses are often moulded, so you can unscrew the arms at the hinges with a small screwdriver. Tempting as it is to thread the shoelaces through these holes, don't, as your necklace will hang downwards, rather than be pert and perky.

You'll need:

- 1 modern pair of moulded sunglasses
- Drill
- 2 mm drill bit
- Shoelaces or cord
- Superglue
- Needlework scissors

Get the drill out. Handily these types of glasses have a lot of frame, and no internal metalwork, so you can drill straight through the frames.

Drill a hole each side of the frame with a 2 mm drill bit, or slightly larger depending on the laces you find.

Here's where we get fancy with knots. The hangman's noose is the one you'll be using.

Getting the tension right can be tricky at first, but with a bit of practise, it'll all be fine. Thread the cord through the hole in one side of the glasses.

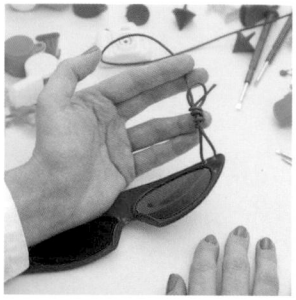

The leading end should be 150 mm. Hold the loop about 50 mm away from the glasses, and wrap the leading end around the two strands of cord, two times, working downwards. And on the third turn bring the leading end through the loop at the top, from behind. Holding the leading end firmly, push your newly made coils upwards; this closes up the loop, and traps the leading end, so it won't come undone.

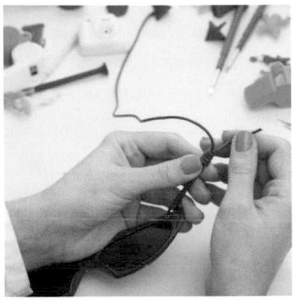

Then pull the coils back towards the frame by tugging on the long length of cord.

Do exactly the same on the other side.

Now we're moving onto slidey knots. These knots will adjust your necklace. We're using two different-coloured cords to make it easier to understand, but once you've grasped the technique you can use any colour you like.

We'll start at the blue end. Fold the blue end back 100mm, then lay it parallel to the red cord, so that the two cut ends are next to each other.

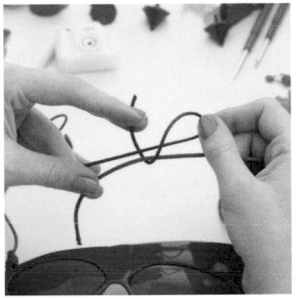

Wrap the blue end around the blue and red cord three times. On the fourth, thread it through the loop at the top, from behind.

Next, push the coils upwards, pulling on the long blue cord, until the blue cord is trapped. You'll know if you've done it right if the red cord moves freely through the knot. Be careful not to pull it right through, or all your knottiness will be undone.

We have a borderline obsession with finding things with ladies' faces on.

Now we're heading for the red cord. Fold the red end back on itself by 100mm, and wrap it around three times. On the fourth, thread it through the loop at the top, from behind.

Then push the coils upwards, as before, pulling on the long red cord. Again, make sure it's good and tight.

You should now have two slidey knots.

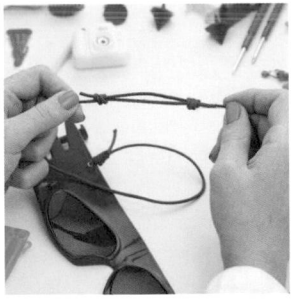

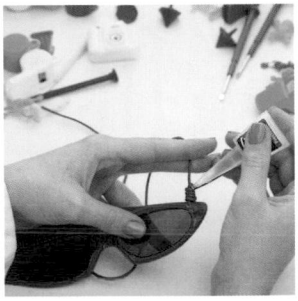

Now get the superglue out.

On the knots next to the glasses, spot some superglue on the reverse of the knot, where the leading end is poking out. The glue secures the knot and it'll stop the cord fraying when you cut it. Let the glue dry.

When the glue's dry, go ahead and neatly snip, with the needlework scissors, the excess of the cord, so that you get a nice, neat, stubby knot.

On the slidey knots put a tiny touch of superglue on the loose ends close to the knots. DON'T glue the moving cord.

Let the glue dry, and snip off the excess.

A final word

It's the end of our book, but, hopefully, the start of your adventure. You've got all the techniques in hand, now it's all about giving it a go.

It can be a bit scary to embark on your own, so enlist a few like-minded friends and head to your nearest charity shop or car boot, collect some treasure and spend an afternoon creating some heading-out-on-the-town jewellery. Hopefully the book will have inspired you, but so will your friends. Sharing ideas, looking over each other's shoulders, experimenting, suggesting what looks good with what is all part of the fun – and you never know where it'll lead!

After we left college, we had a few ideas, a lot of enthusiasm, and a great bunch of friends. We enlisted them when we had to make our first collection on that mad weekend twelve years ago, chatting in a sunny garden about all the things that we could make. And because we talked non-stop about Tatty Devine we made more friends who inspired us to try new things, or collaborated with us on some our favourite projects. At the Cast-Off knitting club, we dropped stitches, and at the Mangle studios we got bonkers images printed on belts and purses and met artist Rob Ryan, who makes the most romantic, intricate paper cuts. He wanted to make a piece of jewellery that described what was in his heart, and he made us think what was in our hearts, which was the loveliest thing to think about; we've worked with him ever since. And we jumped at the chance to work with band Belle and Sebastian; their music has been the sound track to our lives, so making a Dog on Wheels brooch was like a dream come true.

When we started we would never have imagined that we'd have two shops, an on-line boutique, and that we'd be stocked in over 200 shops worldwide. One of our most popular pieces is the name necklace. We first made these as Christmas presents for all of the friends who helped us out; other people saw them and wondered where they could get them from, so we started making them to sell. Now even Katy Perry has one. But we still love the same things that we've always loved –putting on art shows in the Brick Lane shop, buying records, skip diving and making things. And there's nothing stopping you doing the same sort of things – like putting on an exhibition in your bedroom or in a pop-up tent in the garden, making a piece of hand-made jewellery as a birthday gift or designing a birthday card and getting busy with the glitter.

We know that nothing beats the satisfaction of getting the glue gun out or the drill and creating something genius.

We'd love to see what you've come up with! Send us pictures of your makes, tells us what inspires you and where you wore your latest, newly created piece of jewellery.

And it doesn't matter if it all goes wrong. Sometimes mistakes lead to the best inventions, but help is at hand if you want to try and rescue something or are stuck on a fiddly technique, head to our website for practical advice.

Inspiration is everywhere; all you need to do is go and look for it! So are you ready to begin exploring?

Here's our online address: www.tattydevine.com.

Crafty shopping with Tatty Devine

We've said it before and we'll say it again: 'One girl's rubbish is another girl's treasure'

... so we are constantly visiting car boots, charity shops, and flea markets, rummaging through old stuff, on the look out for random junk that can be transformed into something cool. Check out websites like www.yourbooty.co.uk for your nearest car boot, and be prepared to get up nice and early to get the best stuff. You could even go on a charity shop crawl. Canvas an area, get on train, wear comfortable shoes, eat chips for tea.

We LOVE:

♣ Battersea Car boot, Battersea Tec College, Battersea Park Rd, London - Sundays

♦ Hook Rd Arena, Epsom - Mega bank holiday Monday extravaganza

♠ Rousdon cat boot, Rousdon, Dorset

♣ Dalston Oxfam, 514-518 Kingsland Rd London

♥ Snoopers paradise, 7-8 Kensington Gardens, Brighton

♣ Pam's second hand shop, Priory Lane, Bridport, Dorset

Markets

♦ Thursday at Spitalfields market, London

♠ Camden Passage market, London - stalls on Wednesdays and Saturdays

♥ Porte de Clignancourt flea market, officially called Les Puces de Saint-Ouen, but known to everyone as Les Puces (The Fleas) in Paris

♣ Moritzplatz , 10969 Berlin - Kreuzberg flea market in Berlin

♦ Brick Lane market, London - Sundays go off the beaten track to find people selling off the floor.

♠ The waste market, Kingsland Rd, E8, on the A10 between Middleton Rd and Richmond Rd - Saturdays

Sometimes if we're on the look out for something really special we'll head to vintage shops like:

♥ The Girl Can't Help It, in Alfies Antique Market, 13-25 Church St, London

♣ What the Butler Wore, 131 Lower Marsh, Waterloo, London

♦ Beyond Retro, 110-112 Cheshire St, London

♠ Black out II, 51 Endell St, Covent Garden, London

♥ Cenci, 4 Nettlefold Place, London

For inspiration and a sound track to your days head to bookshops and record stores:

♣ Scoob, 66 Brunswick centre off Marchmont St, London

♦ Animal Aid and advice Charity bookshop, 203 Blackstock Rd, London

♠ Baggins Book Bazaar, 19 High Street, Rochester

♥ Mono, 12 Kings Court, Glasgow

♣ Rough Trade, Drays Walk, London

♦ Piccadilly records, 53 Oldham St , Manchester

Jewellery Findings

Even though you can buy all sorts of findings online, on sites like:

www.beadworks.co.uk
www.creativebeadcraft.co.uk

It's sometimes nice to have a feel of the beads, crystals and sew-on gems before you purchase, so head to:

♠ Beadworks, Tower St, London

♥ Creative Beadcraft, 1 Marshall St, London

Craft Supplies

♣ Prick Your Finger, 260 Globe Rd, London - a shop that is a work of art. They sell amazing hand spun yarns and all kind of ribbons, buttons and various vintage haberdashery.

♦ Fred Aldous, 37 Lever St, Manchester
www.fredaldous.co.uk
has been around for a hundred years and has everything in the crafty universe.

Tools

Most bead and craft shops sell tools, but you can get more specialist stuff at:

♣ H S Walsh, 44 Hatton Gardens, London – diamond drill bits, pendant drills, and all manner of jewellery making equipment.
www.hswalsh.com

Chains

You could up-cycle old jewellery from bargain bins and charity shops. And if you're craving something a little luxurious your local jeweller will have gold and silver chain in different lengths and styles. You can buy plain necklaces in most bead shops, but if you want something heavier and chunkier then DIY stores are a good bet. While you're in there stock up on sand paper, varnish, drill bits, brushes and glues. Often jewellery findings are too delicate for the oversize trinkets we loved to make and the DIY shop often proved to be the answer. Make friends with them, they may have all kinds of weird old stuff hidden away.

We like: Emjay Décor, 263 Bethnal
♦ Green Rd, Bethnal Green

Plectrums

♠ Regent Sound, Denmark St. They sell amazing plectrums, but you can also buy online at
www.guitarplectrums.co.uk

Art supplies, Glitter fabric and leather

♦ Atlantis, Britannia House 68 – 80 Hanbury St London – a real treasure trove of all things arty
www.atlantisart.co.uk

♥ www.josyrose.com
has a brilliant selection of glitter fabric, and they have MASSES of colours to choose from.

Most local fabric shops sell leather, and they sometimes have bags of scraps, which might just do for a cuff. Pop along with your template if you're unsure of the size. eBay is good bet for a cheap and cheerful leather purchase, or for full skins try
♣ www.pittardsleather.co.uk

Beeswax

We brought our block from a food festival in Bridport, but a beeswax candle would do the job too.

Stationery Shops

We love jubilee tags, bull dog clips, coloured drawing pins and split pin fasteners. And they are brilliant for lamination too.

♦ We use: Newman's Stationary 324 Bethnal Green Rd,

Other fun shops

Poundshops have all manner of household goods and tools at bargain prices. Look out for brightly coloured tape measures and crafty stuff too.

♥ Party Party 9-13 Ridley Rd, Dalston
www.thepartypartyshop.com
has all kinds of party bag toys. Head upstairs and check out their great selection of cake decorations.

Pet Shops

You can find old bells and plastic toys meant for budgie, and day-glo ping-pong balls for cats, in a forgotten corner of a pet shop. Snap them up, and transform them into cool pendants or earrings.

Corner shops

Great for cheap, shrinkable crisp packets or for unusually packaged imports.

♣ Also try
www.cybercandy.co.uk
for sweets wrappers with good graphics

Index

A

acrylic glasses necklaces 102–15
- pearl 102–3, 108–11
- simple 106–7
- snazzy sunglasses 112–15

Araldite 54

B

backings, suede 46, 48, 64–5
badges 13
barrettes (hair slides) 27
- tape measure rosette 75

bead caps 26
beading silks 26
beads 23
beeswax 22, 85, 94–5
Belle and Sebastian 116
belts, tape measure rosette 76
blinging clip-on shades 63, 66–7
bow tie necklace 38–41
bra-slider ties 47, 49
bracelets
- leather cuff 42–3
- musical note charm 83
- photocopy watch 50–1
- plectrum 86–9, 91

brass
- necklaces 82
- rings 60–1

Brick Lane shop 42, 64, 92, 116
brooches
- backs 27
- clasp safety tips 55
- glitter stars and heart 62, 64–5
- radio 45, 54–5
- sausage dog 58–9
- tape measure rosette 72–6

brushes 20

C

callotes 26
chains 25
- acrylic glasses necklace 106–7
- ball 25
- basic necklace 36
- belcher 25
- curb 25
- cutting 36
- fruit machine dice necklace 99–101
- keyboard necklace 92–3
- leaders 37
- plectrum bracelet and necklace 86–9
- thickness 34
- trace 25

charms 23
- musical note charm bracelet 83

clip ons 27
craft knives 20
crimp beads 26
crisp packet shrinky necklace 77–9
crystals 23
- acrylic glasses necklaces 107
- blinging clip-on shades 63, 66–7

cufflinks 27
cuffs, leather 42–3

D

D-loops 95
Danish oil 98
drill bits 19, 85
drills 19
    projects 86–115
    technique 84–5

E

earrings, jigsaw puzzle stud 68–9
embellishments 23
eye pins 25

F

files 19
findings 14, 24–7
finger puppets 12
fish hooks 27
food packet shrinky necklace 77–81
fruit machine dice necklace 99–101

G

gems 23
    gem hair band 44, 46–9
glass stopper pendants 56–7
glitter stars and heart brooch 62, 64–5
glue 21
    Araldite 54
    removing 53
    technique 53
glue guns 21, 59
googly eyes 23

H

hacksaws 20
hair band, gem 44, 46–9
hair slides (barrettes) 27
    tape measure rosette 75
hammers 19
head pins 25
heart and stars glitter brooch 62, 64–5
hole punches 18
hole-y-moley necklace 70–1
horse brass necklace 82

J

jewellery wire 22
jigsaw puzzle earrings 68–9
jump rings 24
    for basic necklaces 36
    and chain thickness 34
    and leaders 37
    opening 36

K

keyboard necklace 92–3
keying 53
kilt pins 26
knitting needles 21
knives 20
knots 114–15

L

lamination 50–1
leaders 37
leather
    cuffs 42–3
    gem hair band 44, 46–9
    ties 47, 49
lobster clasps 25, 34

M

mushroom necklace, wooden 96–8
musical note charm bracelet 83

N

necklaces
    acrylic glasses 102–15
    basic 36
    bow tie 38–41
    fruit machine dice 99–101
    glass stopper pendants 56–7
    hole-y-moley 70–1
    keyboard 92–3
    palette 82
    plectrum 86–9
    shrinky 77–81
    tape measure rosette 75
    threepenny bit 90, 94–5
    wooden mushroom 96–8
needles 21, 22

O

O'Connor, Erin 46

P

palette necklace 82
pearl acrylic glasses necklace 102–3, 108–11
pendants
    glass stopper 56–7
    mounts 26
Perry, Katy 116
photocopy watch bracelet 50–1
pianos, toy, necklace 92–3
pins 21
plectrum bracelet and necklace 86–9, 91
pliers 18

R

radio brooch 45, 54–5
ribbons
    rosettes 76
    ties 47, 49
ring shanks 27
rings, sovereign 60–1, 90
rosettes, tape measure 72–6
Ryan, Rob 116

S

safety pins 26
Sam Brown studs 26
sausage dog brooch 58–9
saws 20
scalpels 20
scissors 20
screw drivers 19
screw in eyelets 25
scribe and braddle 20
sequins 23
shades, blinging clip-on 63, 66–7
shoelaces 96–8, 114–15
sovereign rings 60–1, 90
Stanley knives 20
stars and heart glitter brooch 62, 64–5
storage 14–17
studs 27
suede backings 46, 48, 64–5
sunglasses, snazzy necklace 112–15

T

tape measures 21
    rosettes 72–6
templates 42–3
thimbles 21
threepenny bit necklace 90, 94–5
ties
    bra-slider 47, 49
    leather 47, 49
    ribbon 47, 49
tools 14, 18–23
tweezers

V

varnish 68–9
Velcro fastenings 51
Vogue magazine 46

W

watch bracelet, photocopy 50–1
weights 60–1
wire cutters 18
wooden mushroom necklace 96–8

THE
BEST
OF

STOP